JAKE WILSON

Jake Wilson was born in London in 1978 and grew up in Melbourne, where he works as a freelance writer. Formerly a co-editor of *Senses of Cinema* (www.sensesofcinema.com), he is currently a regular film reviewer for the Melbourne *Age* and the *Sydney Morning Herald*. This is his first book.

To Nikki

mad dog morgan

JAKE WILSON

CURRENCY PRESS,
SYDNEY

First published by Currency Press Pty Ltd and the NFSA in 2015.

Currency Press Pty Ltd
PO Box 2287, Strawberry Hills
NSW 2012 Australia
enquiries@currency.com.au
www.currency.com.au

National Film and Sound Archive
GPO Box 2002, Canberra
ACT 2601 Australia
www.nfsa.gov.au

Australian Screen Classics series: ISSN 1447-557X

Cataloguing-in-Publication data for this title is available from the National Library of Australia website: www.nla.gov.au

Cover design by Emma Vine for Currency Press.
Printed by Fine Print and Copy Service, St Peters, NSW.
All images within the text are reproduced with the kind permission of Philippe Mora and John Webb.
All photographs from the set of *Mad Dog Morgan* were taken by Angus Forbes. Unless otherwise stated in the caption, the images in the book are sourced from the National Film and Sound Archive.
Front cover shows Dennis Hopper as Mad Dog Morgan. (Photo: Angus Forbes)
Back cover image shows illustration of Morgan. (Photo courtesy of Philippe Mora)

AUSTRALIAN SCREEN CLASSICS

JANE MILLS
Series Editor

Our national cinema plays a vital role in our cultural heritage and in showing us at least something of what it is to be Australian. But the picture can get blurred by unruly forces such as competing artistic aims, inconstant personal tastes, political vagaries, constantly changing priorities in screen education and training, technological innovation and the market.

When these forces remain unconnected, the result can be an artistically impoverished cinema and audiences who are disinclined to seek out and derive pleasure from a diverse range of films, including Australian ones.

This series is a part of screen culture which is the glue needed to stick these forces together. It's the plankton in the moving image food chain that feeds the imagination of our filmmakers and their audiences. It's what makes sense of the opinions, memories, responses, knowledge and exchange of ideas about film.

Above all, screen culture is informed by a love of cinema. And it has to be carefully nurtured if we are to understand and appreciate the aesthetic, moral, intellectual and sentient value of our national cinema.

Australian Screen Classics will match some of our best-loved films with some of our most distinguished writers and thinkers, drawn from the worlds of culture, criticism and politics. All we ask of our writers is that they feel passionate about the films they choose. Through these thoughtful, elegantly-written books, we hope that screen culture will work its sticky magic and introduce more audiences to Australian cinema.

Jane Mills is Associate Professor in Communication in the School of Communication and Creative Industries at Charles Sturt University.

CONTENTS

This is Morgan's country: now steady, Bill.
(Stunted and grey, hunted and murderous.)
Squeeze for the first pressure. Shoot to kill.

Morgan's Country, Francis Webb

Prologue: The Dream

Water plummets onto rock, exploding in whiteness without sound. Downstream, the torrent slows, glistening in the sun. From somewhere comes the drone of a didgeridoo.

Mad blue eyes stare petrified at nothing.

No, not at nothing... at a vision. In a waterhole at the foot of a cliff a liquid crater forms, spray rising from the centre. But instead of expanding, the ripples contract.

The eyes widen. Down a steep slope, crackling fire pours like lava.

The crater narrows to a point; a man emerges feet first and shoots up like a rocket, boots pointing skyward, body aflame.

The burning man rises parallel to the cliff-face, twisting upright in mid-air, stretching out his arms like wings. The flames on his body are mirrored in the water below.

The eyes close.

At the top of the cliff, a second man is waiting. As his double approaches, he stumbles and falls. The burning man leaps on the other like a wolf recognising its prey.

1. The Morgan Legend

This is a book about stories, and about what happens when one story is mapped onto another. Mostly these stories concern three men, the bushranger Daniel Morgan, the filmmaker Philippe Mora and the actor Dennis Hopper. Each in his own way made a central contribution to *Mad Dog Morgan* (1976)—one of the best Australian films of its era, and one that came into being under circumstances so strange it is sometimes hard to believe it exists at all.

Mad Dog is a multilayered text in its own right, enriched by many paradoxes and contradictions: a film quintessentially Australian yet conscious of its place in world cinema, set in the colonial past yet steeped in the radicalism of the 1970s, horrified yet exultant in its view of violent resistance, and indebted to a wide range of cultural traditions high and low. Morgan himself is portrayed as a ruthless avenger, yet also as a helpless victim, prefiguring the antiheroic outlaw protagonists of such later Australian films as *The Chant of Jimmie Blacksmith* (1978), *Bad Boy Bubby* (1993) and *Chopper* (2000). In its vivid messiness and hysteria, its refusal to smooth over the fault-lines of Australian history, *Mad Dog* feels singular yet representative of something larger than itself—which is one definition of a classic.

As a dramatisation of Morgan's career, *Mad Dog* contains both truth and fiction. So, unavoidably, does this book. There are many stories about Morgan, and many more about the *Mad Dog* shoot: in both cases, it is sometimes impossible to separate the way it was from the way it merely should have been.

'When the legend becomes fact, print the legend', a newspaper editor famously says at the end of John Ford's *The Man Who Shot Liberty Valance* (1962). But the relationship between fact and legend is a complex one—something which Ford, as it happens, understood extremely well. The same can be said of Mora, whose recent surrealistic essay films such as *Absolutely Modern* (2012) continue his career-long effort to tap into history's unconscious, the madness beneath the dry official recital.

This book proceeds on a similar basis: while sticking to the facts as far as possible, I've assumed that conjectures and even fantasies are as meaningful and worthy of preservation as whatever passes for truth. If this seems irrational, I can only say that history, like cinema, depends on a faith that can hardly be rationally justified: that in some sense it is possible to wind back the clock and restore the past to life.

One of the things we know for sure is that his name wasn't Morgan. Most likely he started life as John or Jack Fuller, though his biographer Margaret Carnegie identified him as William Moran; either way, it's agreed that he was born around 1830 in the Macarthur region of New South Wales, and that his parents were Irish-Catholic, probably ex-convicts. It is said that as a child he had an intense fear of darkness; that he loved horses, and exerted a strange power over them; that he used to spend days at a time alone in the bush, surviving on possums and grubs. How he came to be known as 'Daniel Morgan' is a mystery; the nicknames 'Mad Dog' and 'Mad Dan' did not come into use till after his death.[1]

As a young man, Morgan made his way to Castlemaine, one of the boom towns of the Victorian gold rush then in full swing. Quite likely he tried his luck as a miner, but his first claim to public attention dates from April 1854, when he bailed up a small group of men at a shepherd's hut. The story about this is characteristic: it's said that he tied up two of his victims then returned an hour later to bring them some blankets (which, being tied up, they couldn't reach). For this crime, he was sentenced to twelve years hard labour—the judge was Redmond Barry, who would later order the hanging of Morgan's famous successor Ned Kelly—and sent to a prison hulk moored at Williamstown just outside Melbourne.

In June 1860 Morgan was released early for good behaviour, but by the middle of 1863 he had launched on his bushranging career in earnest. Dozens of armed robberies were attributed to him, gaining him notoriety throughout the Riverina—the pastoral region of New South Wales where he based himself—and on the other side of the Murray river in Victoria. His appearance added to his legend: one eyewitness described him as a tall man with an immense black beard, and a hooked nose that gave him the look of a ferocious bird of prey.

'An immense black beard': Dennis Hopper as Daniel Morgan.

Without question Morgan could be erratic, alarming, even sadistic. He is believed to have killed at least three men; he liked to spray bullets around carelessly, and to set haystacks and wool bales on fire. Yet the image of a crazed monster, encouraged by the newspapers, was not the whole story. Though less politically articulate than Kelly, Morgan likewise served to some degree as a champion of the people—the rural labourers and small farmers, often of Irish heritage, who struggled to assert themselves against the Anglo-Australian ruling class. On one occasion he bailed up the Burrumbuttock sheep station and forced the owner, Thomas Gibson, to write cheques for all his employees (despite Morgan's threats, Gibson had them cancelled before they were cashed).

Clearly Morgan wanted people to like him, though without quite believing that they did. One account says he was so fearful of being poisoned that even from seeming well-wishers he would accept no food but hard-boiled eggs; it is hard to say if that speaks of sensible caution or paranoia. Compared to most bushrangers he was a lone wolf: he had his network of riding companions and informants—both white and Aboriginal—but never a regular gang. Yet he showed an almost neurotic concern for his reputation, on one occasion coming out of hiding to complain to a pub landlord about unfair reports in the press. 'Publish what you like', he said, 'but don't make the devil blacker than he really is'.

While Morgan's final night on earth is not as famous as Kelly's last stand at Glenrowan, it adds a similar touch of poetry to his myth.[2] On April 8, 1865, Morgan bailed up Peechelba Station near Wangaratta, the home of the Macpherson family. All those present were held hostage, but Morgan allowed a nursemaid, Alice Keenan, to slip away to tend to a sick child; with aid from another servant, she sent for help. In the meantime, Morgan ordered one of the young women of the household to play the piano. Listening to the music, he grew sentimental, remarking that he was often out in the bush for weeks without meeting a living soul; that he would not have committed his murders if circumstance had not forced his hand; that he was innocent of the crime he had been jailed for, but now meant to be revenged on mankind for ever.

After supper the women and children were allowed to go to bed, while Morgan stayed up all night with the station owner Ewan Macpherson drinking whisky; early the next morning he washed his face, groomed his hair and beard, and demanded a horse, which he promised to return. He then stepped outdoors, seemingly unaware that a group of troopers and armed vigilantes lay in wait. Their plan was to capture him alive, but on his way to the stables he was shot in the back by a servant named John Wendlan, dying a few hours later.

That was the end of Morgan, but not of his story. Although the coroner William Dobbyn returned a verdict of 'justifiable homicide', Melbourne's *Age* newspaper declared bluntly that 'Morgan was lynched'. There was an outcry, too, over the treatment of the corpse, which was sent to Wangaratta where it was briefly put on public display. Locks of hair were taken as souvenirs, and the Police Superintendent Francis Cobham ordered the flaying of the beard, which he reportedly planned to turn into a tobacco pouch; another version of the story maintains that the pouch was made from the tanned skin of Morgan's scrotum. While this latter rumour did not appear in print till much later, a report from a correspondent of the *Wangaratta Despatch* was almost equally lurid:

> Decapitation, hacking, wrenching, cutting, skinning, fleshing and boxing up, seem to have been indulged in as a pastime or recreation; and those by whom the body should have been

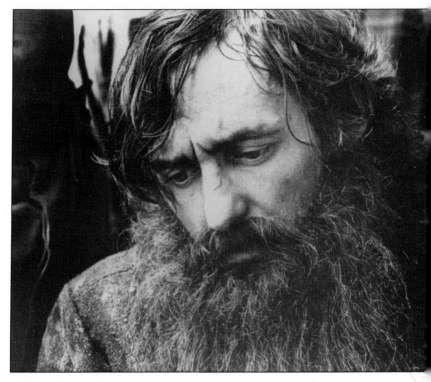

Hopper's Morgan in sorrowful mood.

held as sacred, and, while in their possession, jealously guarded
against any desecration, calmly looked on, or became principals
in atrocities which make humanity shudder.

Finally, Dobbyn had Morgan's head sent down to the
University of Melbourne to be inspected by Professor Halford of
the Department of Anatomy who was known to take an interest
in the criminal brain. When all this came out in public, Dobbyn
was suspended from duty, and Cobham lost two months' pay for

(as the *Ovens and Murray Advertiser* put it) 'so ruthlessly denuding Morgan of his hirsute appendages'.

If Morgan was famous in his lifetime, he became even more so thereafter. Ballads glorified or damned him; he was portrayed in waxwork, on the stage, and in serialised adventure stories such as *Morgan, The Mail Robber; or, The Bandits of the Bush!* In Rolf Boldrewood's *Robbery Under Arms*, the most famous of all bushranging novels, he appears as the brutish Dan Moran, a portrait that no doubt helped cement the prevailing view of him as a heartless demon. Still today, his legend endures: at Hanging Rock in Victoria two landmarks are named after him—Morgan's Lookout and Morgan's Blood Waterfall—and his ghost is said to haunt the area, though there is little evidence he ever came near it.

It was not till the mid-twentieth-century that Morgan would receive truly perceptive literary treatment. In 1950, the poet Francis Webb published 'Morgan's Country', a powerful evocation of Morgan's troubled state of mind in his final hours. This Morgan is 'mad' in the fullest sense, possibly schizophrenic, a condition which Webb, who spent his own life in and out of mental hospitals, evokes with intense empathy:

> The grey wolf at his breakfast. He cannot think
> Why he must make haste, unless because their eyes
> Are poison at every well where he might drink.
> Unless because their gabbling voices force
> The doors of his grandeur, first terror, then only hate.
> Now terror again. Dust swarms under the doors.

Before moving on to what a later generation made of Morgan, there is one other incident worth mentioning. In 1895 a young lawyer and his fiancée visited the Macpherson family at Dagworth Station, their property in central Queensland; the couple were especially friendly with the manager's sister Christina Macpherson, said to have been the sick child Alice Keenan left to tend to that night at Peechelba. To amuse the visitors, Christina played a tune on the zither which she had heard at the races; in return, the lawyer wrote a new set of lyrics, about a thief who prefers to die than face arrest, and whose ghost haunts the region forever more. The lawyer, of course, was 'Banjo' Paterson, and the song was *Waltzing Matilda*.

11. Morgan and Others

As a boy, Philippe Mora was fascinated by bushrangers; in this he was a typical Australian child of the 1950s, although in other respects he was anything but. He was born in Paris in 1949; two years later his family arrived in Melbourne, where his parents Georges and Mirka brought a dash of European colour to a still largely monocultural city. Georges established himself as a restaurateur and art dealer; Mirka became known for her symbolist paintings of animals, children, and strange hybrid creatures, most of them with huge, dark eyes.

Among the Mora family's kindred spirits in Australia were the art patrons John and Sunday Reed, the nucleus of the famous Heide Circle, named for their home at a former dairy farm northeast of Melbourne. Many artists came to Heide over the years, including the painter Sidney Nolan, who was Sunday's lover in the 1940s before he married John Reed's sister Cynthia and settled in London; the Ned Kelly paintings that would make him famous were left behind in the corridors of Heide, where the young Mora would encounter them a few years later.

These paintings were deliberately 'primitive': Kelly's famous iron helmet was rendered as a plain black rectangle with a slot like a letterbox, dotted with wary eyes or simply revealing the blue sky beyond. This was the bushranger as modernist icon: abstract but also cartoonish, capable of bearing any meaning or none. No wonder the character became 'as big as Batman' for the children at Heide, who used to dress up as the Kelly gang and run round the garden chasing the chickens.

While the Reeds avoided discussing Nolan, for the Moras the past was more generally taboo—understandably, as there was plenty that Georges and Mirka might wish to forget. Georges had started life as Günther Morawski, born in Leipzig to a well-off Jewish family of Polish descent; he studied medicine in Berlin in the early 1930s, fleeing to France when the Nazis came to power and going on to fight in the Resistance. Mirka, born in Paris, was still a teenager during the war; in all probability she would have ended up in Auschwitz if her father hadn't managed to bribe officials to get his family released from a transit camp. In her autobiography, Mirka describes the traumatic memory of riding away from the camp in a cart, looking back at the remaining prisoners staring at her from behind the barbed wire—prototypes for the sad-eyed creatures who have gazed out from her paintings ever since.

Painting was in Mora's blood, and from his early teens he began to experiment with filmmaking as well, inspired by the 'anti-art' of Dada and surrealism; as he would later recognise, these movements also represented a response to trauma, in this case that of the First World War. In the late 1960s he found his way to London, moving into The Pheasantry, a Chelsea mansion which housed a number of Australian countercultural luminaries including the Pop artist Martin Sharp as well as Germaine Greer, then at work on *The Female Eunuch*. Among the occasional visitors were the Beatles' George Harrison and the then-fashionable 'anti-psychiatrist' R.D. Laing, who believed that madness was really sanity, and would observe the goings-on at The Pheasantry as if seeking confirmation of that view.

Mora had to make an effort to stand out in this milieu, mounting exhibitions with titles such as *Anti-Social Realism* and *Vomart*, as well as assorted Happenings (one involved selling baby rats in editions of eight). Soon he had completed his first feature film, *Trouble in Molopolis* (1969): a zany Brechtian musical financed by his rock star friend Eric Clapton, starring a mentally ill tramp named John Ivor Golding as a Hitler-style dictator. Encouraged to improvise, Golding gave an effective performance, but reportedly disgraced himself at the premiere by defecating in the front row.

As a follow-up, Mora planned to shoot a comic-book burlesque, *The Phantom versus the Fourth Reich*; the script caught the eye of the Hitler-obsessed comic Peter Sellers who, inviting Mora to visit him at home, opened the door dressed as the Führer. Presuming stars were entitled to eccentricity, Mora took the costume in his stride. Though the project soon fell apart, it somehow led to the documentary *Swastika* (1974), centred on home movies of Hitler, Eva Braun and their circle. At the Cannes Film Festival premiere, fights are said to have broken out: was Mora trying to excuse evil by showing the human face of a monster?

A second compilation documentary followed, *Brother Can You Spare a Dime* (1975), about America in the Depression. After this, Mora—still only in his mid-twenties—resolved to make a more ambitious feature, with his friend Jeremy Thomas on board as producer. The pair set their sights on Australia, where government intervention had revived the film industry after decades of inactivity. But what subject to choose? Bushranger films had been central to Australian cinema in the earliest silent days, and though

Mora in the late 1960s. A friend described him as 'a short, dark, precocious youth'.
(Photo: Bob Seidemann)

the genre was killed off by censorship in the 1910s there seemed
no reason why it too should not be revived. Thinking back to
Nolan's paintings, Mora would have been tempted to try a Kelly
film of his own, if the British director Tony Richardson hadn't
got in first with his disastrous 1970 effort starring Mick Jagger.

Fortuitously, Mora was sent a copy of *Morgan, The Bold
Bushranger*, a newly-published study by Margaret Carnegie—
another art patron and friend of the Mora family, who had taken
to the writing of history in later life. The story had everything:
violence, psychology, the opportunity for urgent topical treatment.

Mora wrote the screenplay on the boat back to Melbourne from London, stopping off briefly in Cape Town where a glimpse of the apartheid system encouraged him to use the outcast figure of Morgan to explore the theme of racial persecution. In terms of plot he stuck close to Carnegie's book, adding a few baroque touches such as having Morgan raped in prison.

Two challenges lay ahead. The first was funding, to be obtained mostly from private sources. Georges Mora helped, as did Carnegie who also allowed Mora to shoot at her family property on the Riverina; other connections came about through Thomas whose father Ralph was a well-known director in the United Kingdom. The second was to sign an internationally bankable star. The first choice was Stacy Keach, but Keach's agent was discouraging: 'Stacy's very successful at the moment, and I don't think he'll want to play this character.' Martin Sheen was also considered, but no contract was signed. Then Mora thought of Dennis Hopper.

Hopper's connection to outlaw mythology went back a long way. He was born in 1936 in Dodge City, Kansas, famous as the rowdy Old West town where Wyatt Earp served as assistant marshal. His father was distant, his mother 'a screamer and a yeller'. Much of his time was spent at his grandfather's nearby twelve-acre farm, where dust blew so thickly he had to wear a gas mask to school. Often alone, he found escape in painting, in the movies, and in huffing fumes from the tank of his grandfather's tractor. His early memories could belong to a character from a Terrence Malick film:

> I got a telescope and looked at the sun and went blind for five days. I caught lightning bugs, lightning shows, sunsets, and followed animal tracks in the snow. I had a kite. I used the telescope to burn holes in newspapers. The sun was brighter

than I was. God was everywhere and I was desperate.

The answer to the desperation was Hollywood. As precocious a talent as Mora, Hopper at eighteen was under contract to Warner Brothers—playing his first significant role opposite James Dean in *Rebel Without a Cause* (1955), an experience that would change the course of his life. Dean stood for new-style Method acting, entailing improvisation, the summoning of personal 'sense memories', and no small amount of diva behaviour. To Hopper he became a mentor as well as a friend, preaching the gospel of authenticity above all else: 'Well, if you're going to smoke a cigarette, don't act smoking a cigarette, just smoke it.'

Hopper's mind was duly blown. Swiftly he grew to idolise Dean, much as Dean in turn idolised Marlon Brando; the uncertain border between acting and being became an obsession, especially after Dean's death in a car crash in September 1955. Having already acquired a taste for loose living—drugs, women, reckless driving—Hopper saw himself as the inheritor of Dean's rebel mantle both onscreen and off, even as his career failed to progress beyond playing secondary heavies in Westerns.

Needless to say, Hopper and the 1960s were made for each other. Flitting between New York and Los Angeles, he spent the decade aiming to stay close to the action: studying at the Actors Studio, screen-testing for Andy Warhol, marching with Martin Luther King, and reinventing himself as an art collector and practitioner (first painting, then photography), as well as a figure on the Hollywood social scene. Yet fame remained elusive, till his friend Peter Fonda enlisted him to direct and co-star in *Easy Rider* (1969), a low-budget biker film aimed at the youth market. Unexpectedly, this became a smash hit—touching a generational

James Dean's successor: Hopper as Hollywood outlaw. (Photo: Umbrella Entertainment)

nerve in both its utopianism and its ominous violence, leading up to a climax where the protagonists literally crash and burn.

Bankable as never before, Hopper was able to persuade the generally conservative Universal Studios to back his dream project, the reflexive anti-Western *The Last Movie* (1971). Besides writing and directing, he starred as Kansas, a stuntman working on a Western in Peru which is abandoned after the accidental death of the actor (Dean Stockwell) playing Billy the Kid. Subsequently, a group of Peruvian Indians restage the unfinished film as a religious ritual; seeing Kansas as the logical substitute for the dead man, they set out to sacrifice him in turn.

Though deliberately disorientating, *The Last Movie* is less chaotic than it seems. On one level, as the critic J. Hoberman has noted, it functions as an elegy for Dean, who had himself planned to play a version of Billy the Kid in Arthur Penn's *The Left Handed Gun* (1958). On another, it demands to be seen as a documentary on Hopper himself, living out his role as the quintessential Ugly American abroad. A lurid *LIFE* magazine cover story chronicled the excesses which turned the Peru shoot into a Happening in its own right: bondage parties, peyote overdoses, clashes with the locals culminating in violent brawls.

Once shooting wrapped, Hopper threw himself into a new phase of the adventure, moving into the Mabel Dodge Luhan house in Taos, New Mexico, where D.H. Lawrence had stayed on first coming to the United States. Here he worked feverishly on editing, buying a local cinema to screen his work in progress, while stocking up on weaponry to defend himself from his Hispanic and Native American neighbours, who fought a running battle against the encroaching counterculture.

At the Venice Film Festival premiere of *The Last Movie* response was muted; back home, a disastrous university preview culminated in a female student punching the director in the face, yelling 'You sexist fucking pig!' Fearing the worst, Universal insisted Hopper deliver a more conventionally linear cut. When he declined, the film was dumped, playing in a handful of theatres with minimal promotion. As abruptly as it had started, Hopper's moment in the sun was over—as if by burning up his character at the end of *Easy Rider* he had consigned himself to a living death. For years he stayed in Taos, partying with his hippie entourage and adding to his gun collection. Then came the invitation to go to Australia.

III. Morgan Rides Again

'Chef', bellowed Dennis Hopper, 'there is something suspiciously wrong with my Chiko roll'.

It was midnight at a New South Wales truck stop, halfway through the *Mad Dog* shoot. Hopper was sitting with Jim Oram of Sydney's *Daily Mirror*, the only journalist to report in detail from behind the scenes. Oram's colourful dispatches would launch a tradition of tall tales about the making of *Mad Dog*, encouraged by the fact that Hopper's acting technique itself relied on the blurring of reality and fiction. Indeed, Oram put special emphasis on Hopper's idiosyncratic version of the Method—informing his readers that off-duty the actor continued to live the part of Morgan, speaking in an Irish accent and imbibing vast quantities of Bundaberg rum.

Luring Hopper to Australia had not been difficult. As Thomas later told *Sight and Sound*:

> We went to see his agent, Robert Raison, who had a beautiful house and had been Cole Porter's lover. Lovely guy. He said: 'I love this script. Dennis gets buggered in this script. I want you to go see him.'

Mora remembers getting out of a single-engine plane at the Taos airport and seeing Hopper at the end of the runway holding a rifle: Morgan to the life. In his bullet-riddled pick-up truck, Hopper drove Mora and Thomas to their hotel, advising them not to stay out after midnight: 'That's when the Indians start shooting.' By next day he had agreed to come on board. After an obligatory screening of *The Last Movie*, Mora and Thomas headed off, largely unaware of what they had got themselves into: no-one had warned them that Hopper was effectively blacklisted in Hollywood, and had barely worked for the past three years.

But there was no time for second thoughts, not with a hundred-odd speaking roles to be cast. Mora had always envisaged that the crucial role of Billy—an amalgam of Morgan's various Aboriginal offsiders—would be played by David Gulpilil, the young traditional dancer from Arnhem Land who had impressed many in Nicolas Roeg's *Walkabout* (1971). And clearly, there could be no better choice for the villainous Cobham than Frank Thring, whose brief but illustrious Hollywood career had included the roles of Pontius Pilate in *Ben-Hur* (1959) and Herod in *King of Kings* (1961). For Morgan's other key antagonists, Mora chose actors who were or would become comparably iconic: Jack Thompson, John Hargreaves, Bill Hunter.

As cinematographer, Mora enlisted an old friend, Mike Molloy, who had never shot a feature but had worked as camera operator with Roeg and Stanley Kubrick; the choice was made to shoot in anamorphic Panavision on the grounds that the format would suit the Australian landscape. Filming began in late October of 1975 in the Riverina town of Holbrook, with the production base shifting after a few weeks to Beechworth in north-east Victoria. The budget was under half a million dollars: impossibly modest for a project of such scope.

Little was glamorous about the shoot. Thomas maintains that

the crew would strike if they weren't given beer for breakfast; Mora is fond of saying that catering consisted of 'barbecuing a whole sheep'. Authentic locations were used where possible, including a remote cave in the Yambla Ranges which Morgan was said to have used as a hideout; watching crew members lug heavy lighting equipment up the mountain made Mora think of the Second World War.

There were many other challenges. In the first week, the area experienced its heaviest rains in years, washing away the goldfields set which had to be rebuilt overnight. An entire subplot was scrapped when a dog painted to resemble a thylacine escaped and ran off; for long after, according to Mora, there were rumoured sightings of a mysterious striped creature lurking in the bush... One story that is more certainly apocryphal is that Hopper was arrested soon after arriving in Sydney: *Mad Dog*'s associate producer Richard Brennan swears this never happened, and so does Satya de la Manitou, Hopper's loyal friend and personal assistant.[3]

What no-one denies is that Hopper was a fully fledged alcoholic— he also made heavy use of cocaine, if only to

Hopper and Mora bonding on set.

stay awake and keep drinking—and that directing him had its hazards. During the filming of a difficult scene involving a wind machine and an out-of-control horse, he refused to do a second take, causing Mora public embarrassment. After the two went off into the bush together, Mora was able to calm things down, reassuring

The three musketeers: producer Jeremy Thomas, Hopper and Mora.

Hopper of his love and respect. On another occasion, Hopper flew into a rage at Mora for poking an actor with a stick: 'We're not animals, man, we're not puppets!' As Mora tells it, the actor in question was practically blind, and needed the prod to recognise his cue.

Mora stresses that while the camera was rolling Hopper was essentially a Hollywood professional: still, his gonzo approach did create difficulties here and there. He had trouble with the riding sequences, the quarter horses supplied by Carnegie being a far cry from the tame beasts he was used to in Hollywood. Getting him to stick to his marks was a lost cause, one reason so much of the film is in wide shot. Maintaining continuity was less of a problem, aside from the occasion when Morgan's boots disappeared halfway through a scene. 'I'm Mad Dog Morgan, man,

Hopper on horseback. (Photo: Angus Forbes)

I don't need boots', Hopper is said to have blustered. 'Dennis, this is not a movie about magic boots', Mora replied (or should have). The boots were found in a freezer, where Hopper had put them to get rid of the smell.

Given the unreliability of memory, it is lucky we have David Elfick's making-of documentary *To Shoot a Mad Dog* (1976) as a record of the atmosphere on set: the dazzling bush light, the incessant smoking and drinking, the laidback crew members often without shirts. Playing to Elfick's camera, Hopper makes a joking effort to live up to his 'mad' image, tongue out and eyes bulging; a moment later, he's plucking a cigarette from nowhere with a choirboy smile, then holding up a beer and offering a mock celebrity endorsement. Though he retains his Irish brogue, his intense sociability is a negative image of Morgan's solitude: while clearly in a heightened state, he appears brazenly relaxed, utterly confident in his ability to charm.

The confidence was not misplaced. Despite some initial qualms among Australian actors about the importing of an American lead, a widespread excitement was generated by Hopper and his Method, which went beyond anything previously seen in Australian cinema. Hopper was full of stories, and especially loved to recount his experiences with veteran Hollywood directors like Henry Hathaway and George Stevens; he would also reminisce about James Dean, and, according to Mora, was able to 'become' Dean in an uncanny way. On camera, his wild improvisations could bewilder his co-stars—but as Mora noted at the time, this could be said to benefit the film, which at such moments became a documentary of Hopper genuinely 'freaking people out'.

Not that everyone simply accepted his status as top dog. Jack Thompson told Hopper on their first meeting that he had better do Morgan justice; with due humility, Hopper promised that he would. Likewise, there is general agreement that Hopper was cautious around Thring, either because he deeply respected Thring as an actor, or because Thring—perhaps with the tobacco pouch story in mind, perhaps not—took an unsettling interest in Hopper's crotch.

On the other hand, the soft-spoken Gulpilil was initially wary of Hopper, and nearly everyone remembers Gulpilil's disappearance as one of the central events of the shoot. As Mora tells the story on the *Mad Dog* DVD commentary, a couple of Aboriginal trackers had to be sent into the bush, returning with Gulpilil a day or two later. Afterwards, Mora demanded to know what had happened:

> David said 'I had to ask the kookaburras and the trees about Dennis.' And I said 'Really, what did they say?' And he said: 'Well, the kookaburras and the trees all say that Dennis is crazy, mate.' I said 'David, I could have told you that. Please.'

Gulpilil himself now maintains he doesn't remember why he took off, but speaks with great affection of Hopper and the good times they shared. 'Him and me was a *bastard*', he said gleefully when I spoke to him, observing that the main difference between Hopper and Morgan was that Morgan did not have cigarettes—tobacco or otherwise—hidden on his person at all times.

Another story told by Mora and de la Manitou says that Hopper, with his background in the civil rights struggle, led a successful protest when Gulpilil was denied entrance to a pub. Again, Brennan is sceptical: if anything, he says, the locals were keen to demonstrate their open-minded goodwill. Still, several witnesses attest to clashes between the 'film people' and a portion of the rural population, characterised by the set photographer Angus Forbes as 'lantern-jawed pastoralists and former military men'.

Such tensions were inevitable, in a country divided in a much broader sense. During the filming of a scene of Morgan and Billy setting fire to a barn, Hopper rode up, still in character, shouting 'Who the fuck is Whitlam?' The Australian Prime Minister had just been dismissed, marking the end of an entire progressive era.[4]

There were those who feared Hopper might die before the film was complete. Just in case, Mora asked the artist Ivan Durrant to cast Hopper's face in gelatine and create a mask, enabling another actor to play Morgan in long shot. To explain to Hopper why this was needed, Mora improvised a psychedelic scene where Morgan would look at the sky and see his own head exploding. Hopper was impressed: 'Incredible, man, far out.'

That scene didn't make the final cut, but some of its spirit is present in a surreal dream sequence that does involve another performer playing a mirror image of Morgan: the legendary stuntman Grant Page, who was set on fire before leaping backwards from a 75-foot cliff (in the film the footage is reversed, so the burning Page appears to emerge from the water below). Horrifyingly, this had to be shot twice: the first time Page's protective gel evaporated, burning him severely before he could make the leap. In spite of having Page fall on him, Hopper was unharmed.

To mark the end of the main shoot Hopper felt the need for a ritual, driving to Morgan's last resting place at a cemetery in Wangaratta. Before a small group of witnesses, he poured a bottle of spirits over Morgan's grave, then consumed a second bottle—and, according to Brennan, started to attack other tombs—before speeding away in his car. Soon after, he was picked up by the Victorian police, who thus managed to capture Morgan alive, the task they had failed at a century earlier.

The story goes that after analysis of his blood alcohol levels Hopper was pronounced clinically dead, banned from riding in cars in Victoria either as driver or passenger, and packed off back to the States. This can hardly be literally true, for the records show that on the following Monday he returned to work in Sydney, shooting Morgan's jail scenes at a nineteenth-century fort on Bare Island in Botany Bay. The chief rapist was played by the looming Max Fairchild, an old schoolmate of Mora's who would later appear on stage as Lennie in *Of Mice and Men*. After a few takes, Fairchild complained that he was finding Hopper's exposed buttocks less than arousing. 'No-one's more pleased to hear that than me, Max', Hopper is said to have replied. Soon after he was gone, leaving nothing but legends—and, of course, the film itself.

IV. Morgan Finds a Mate

Jack Thompson stands before a granite wall, dapper in fawn coat and black butterfly tie; speaking in an Irish accent, he introduces himself to the camera. 'I am William Henry Manwaring, and a member of the Victorian Detective Police.'

Like most of the characters in *Mad Dog*, Manwaring was a real person. He took part in that final siege at Peechelba, which he described in a manuscript written shortly after (it was he who compared Morgan to a bird of prey). Several scenes in the film use passages from this manuscript almost verbatim—and were shot at an actual nineteenth-century prison in Beechworth, the town where Manwaring was then stationed.

This is an unusual opening: so unusual, in fact, that it was cut from the version of the film originally released in the United States. Immediately it announces *Mad Dog* as a self-conscious, modernist work—modernism with an Australian inflection being Mora's artistic mother tongue. Thompson's direct address to the camera is a textbook Brechtian alienation effect; the flat, front-on staging recalls the comic strip look of *Made in U.S.A.* (1966) and other films by Jean-Luc Godard, the filmmaker most often credited with bringing Brecht's influence into cinema.

The wail of a didgeridoo carries us into the opening credits, set against prints by the nineteenth-century artist S.T. Gill, known for depictions of the goldfields and other characteristic Australian scenes. The first and most striking in the series shows a dead explorer lying far from civilisation, blood streaming from his emaciated torso; a dog sits by him protectively or possessively, while a wedge-tailed eagle hovers overhead. Further back, the bones of a dead horse are picked over by dingos and birds of prey.

Is the explorer's disputed body that of colonial Australia itself? Something like this allegorical interpretation is encouraged by the subsequent Gill prints, arranged to recapitulate the history of colonisation; at times the juxtapositions suggest direct conflict, as when the image of a group of Aboriginal men about to throw their spears is 'answered' by that of a white hunter aiming his gun. The didgeridoo music, supplied by Gulpilil, hints at Morgan's eventual loyalties: this will not be entirely the story of a rebel without a cause.

Now the main part of the film begins, with the Castlemaine goldfields laid out before us in a deep-focus wide shot: tents spread along the bank of a creek, smoke rising from campfires, prospectors digging or crouched by the water, gums leaning over a bridge in the foreground which a Cobb & Co coach crosses. Morgan is already present in this seemingly tranquil image, though we are unlikely to identify him on first viewing: a tiny figure at the end of the bridge, he stands with hands on hips as if already contemplating a hold-up, then moves away with a hint of reluctance. The next shot gives us a closer look at him as he jogs along beside the coach and descends on a dirt track to the main road, briefly losing his footing and skidding down the bank, then touching his hat as he turns to glance at a friendly dog wandering in circles just behind him.

Morgan now crosses the road behind the coach and ascends the opposite bank; an unsteady handheld shot of him from below, followed by a rule-breaking 180-degree cut, gives a clue to his troubled state of mind. We see him clearly now: a dirty fellow in an unbuttoned shirt, hair falling into his eyes, an anxious, even despondent look. The ensuing sequence brings us further inside his consciousness as he makes his way through the miners' camp, immersed in its sights and sounds: a makeshift bar, a punch-up by the creek, a pig rooting around in the grass.

These things are real within the fiction, but they also form part of Morgan's mental universe, like the temptations of a saint: it is already becoming apparent that his 'madness' consists precisely of an inability to distinguish between inner and outer worlds. Passing the bar without a pause, he raises a hand to fend off an acquaintance who addresses him by name. As he keeps walking, he continues to gesture absently but urgently, as if justifying himself to no-one.

'Philippe Mora's films have always been concerned with insanity', Garry Shead wrote in his 1976 article 'Jesus Was an Outlaw', which remains the best analysis of *Mad Dog* written by anybody. Rather than treating the film as a genre exercise or a historical chronicle, Shead sees Morgan as a symbol of the tortured artist, akin to the visionary outcasts who proliferated elsewhere in Australian culture at this period, notably in the novels of Patrick White. 'The film is constructed like a dream', Shead writes, 'dreams within dreams'.

Shead rightly points out that Mora's artistic roots are in the European avant-garde, especially Surrealism. This is not to ignore the fact that Mora, like many of the original Surrealists, was fascinated with the 'low' art of Hollywood—as he demonstrated in his early critical article 'Mythology of Guts', a study of tough-guy iconography published in one of the first issues of *Cinema Papers*, the Australian film magazine he co-founded before making his way to London. Much in this piece anticipates *Mad Dog*, especially the conflation of two seemingly opposed models of cinematic masculinity: the stoic Westerner in the tradition of John Wayne, and the sensitive, masochistic victim-hero incarnated by younger Method types such as Brando or Dean.

Hopper, the Method Cowboy, was one of the few actors who could be said to belong to both traditions at once. Consciously or not, Mora in *Mad Dog* was putting into practice what he had written years earlier, that 'every actor embodies in his physical presence most of the characteristics of people he has played in the past', and that therefore 'when a director double exposes the actor by recreating his myth in another situation/film, the actors [*sic*] myth is exploited by repetition, so that it becomes extremely powerful'.

What, though, was Hopper's myth? Much of his fame depended on his association with youth, but this was becoming incongruous in an actor pushing forty; after twenty years in the business he had never had a hit vehicle aside from his own *Easy Rider*, and even there he had functioned more as sidekick to Fonda than star. For that matter, many of his most memorable later roles would be as shadow to another man, in films ranging from Wim Wenders' psychological thriller *The American Friend* (1977) to Francis Ford Coppola's Vietnam epic *Apocalypse Now* (1979).

Picking up on this, the French critic Jean-Baptiste Thoret has written eloquently on the theme of the doppelgänger in Hopper's career:

> Characters haunted by their Other, a life possessed by its own
> ghost—as if the tragic death of his role model and friend James
> Dean in September 1955 has summoned up the certainty that

> in Hopper's world a part of the self is always absent (without
> leave) so that making films, playing parts, creating works of
> art always (and perhaps especially) means manufacturing a
> double...

This chimes uncannily with Mora's own 'double exposure'
metaphor, which applies to Hopper with special aptness. As Thoret
writes, few actors seem more haunted by their own alternate
selves, past or potential. This may account in part for what Thoret
describes as Hopper's most distinctive quality as a performer, 'a
kind of tangible oscillation between an intense presence in the
world and its elusion'. Typically, Hopper seems 'not all there'—and
not quite the person we might have expected him to be.

Mora has said he made *Mad Dog* from a 'Marxist' perspective,
holding society to blame for turning Morgan into a crazed thief and
eventual killer. Yet Hopper, ever the individualist, plays Morgan
as 'mad' from the outset; nor is it clear whether the causes of
this madness are social or existential. This ambiguity hangs over
the scene of Morgan's clash with Wendlan (Martin Harris), a
moustachioed bully in a Prussian helmet who stands jabbing a
sword into a sheep carcass, pausing to toss a handful of entrails
at a passing Chinese miner. Standing nearby with a black dog at
his feet, Morgan shies away as the guts fly past him; he angrily
intervenes, knocking Wendlan to the ground. Two themes are
introduced here that will remain in tension throughout the film:
the evil of a society that denies outsiders their humanity, and the
deeper horror of a world where both human and animal bodies
may finally be mere carcasses awaiting consumption.

As Morgan gets talking to an older man, Martin (Gerry
Duggan), we glimpse further sides of his personality. He waves

an axe threateningly as he denounces Wendlan as a 'police pimp' (that is, informer): we are given no way to judge the truth of this possibly paranoid claim, though we will meet Wendlan again down the track. In the meantime, Morgan is quick to put an affectionate arm around his new friend, whom he invites to join him in the camp's Chinatown for a pipe of opium.

This cues one of the most striking moments in Hopper's performance: after inhaling from the pipe, he gazes upward, his face half-bathed in the sunlight that filters through the slats of the opium den. Finally he exhales and giggles, while croaking out his dialogue in fits and starts: 'I find... when you're in the goldfields... it's the best cure... for not finding gold.' Opium dens did flourish on the goldfields, and it's not hard to believe that Morgan would turn to drugs to escape his demons; but the sequence also jolts us out of the narrative, as an extra-textual nod to Hopper's hippie persona.

It's clear by now that Morgan is a disruptive force in more ways than one. The character is defined by his sudden, unpredictable shifts of mood, as if he were trying on various personae in search of one that might fit. But equally, Hopper does not 'fit' the film itself: his Method mannerisms inevitably stand out as anachronistic despite the fact that none of his co-stars are likely to be any nearer the reality of nineteenth century Australia. Paradoxically, then, an acting technique meant to increase emotional immediacy winds up supplying the film's central alienation effect.

Yet at another level the immediacy remains. Like *The Last Movie*, *Mad Dog* asks to be viewed as a documentary about its own making; like the comparably Brechtian history films made around the same period by Jean-Marie Straub and Danièle Huillet,

Hopper relaxes with friend Satya de la Manitou, who appeared as an extra in the opium den scene.

it employs 'authentic' locations and texts without erasing signs of the modern. One of the many doubles of Hopper-as-Morgan haunting the film is Mick Jagger, who had performed so feebly as Ned Kelly; Mora described this as an example of what to avoid, but this didn't stop him borrowing the idea of having a bushranger played by a counterculture icon. Rather, he aimed to succeed where Richardson had failed, using the power of stardom to stage a collision between cultures and eras: in its very lack of cohesion, the film can be seen as an allegory of identity—individual or national—as necessarily incomplete and unresolved, battled over like the explorer's corpse.

Allegory, not myth. The critic Gilberto Perez usefully describes allegory as 'a traditional mode that separates literal and figurative levels': while Hopper's performance may not seem literally plausible, it would be hard to find a better figurative expression of Morgan's fragmented state. Allegory is *about* fragmentation, which is why—as scholars such as Felicity Collins have argued, drawing on the ideas of Walter Benjamin—it is especially useful for addressing traumatic histories which resist being represented in literal terms.

As Benjamin tells us, allegory is discontinuous (unlike myth, which binds everything together). Though literally *Mad Dog* centres on Australia's colonial past, figuratively it is not restricted to any one place and time: the Prussian racist Wendlan unmistakably evokes the Nazi era, and by the time we reach the opium den the frame of reference has shifted once more. The mingling of races, the simultaneous solitude and communion of the drug users, the freedom of desire suggested by a glimpse of two women sleeping naked in each others' arms: all of this allegorises the makeshift, marginal utopias of the 1960s, as well as the dream of a future nation perhaps never to be born.

V. Morgan Descending

Swiftly, the dream ends. As the sun sets, armed rioters burst into the opium den, setting it on fire and indiscriminately blasting away. Among them we recognise Wendlan, who calls Martin a 'Chinese-loving bastard' and shoots him in the head. A surreal close-up shows Martin's half-obliterated face; roused from his trance, Morgan bursts into horrified tears.

Much of *Mad Dog*'s reputation for extremity derives from this single sequence, where the shock is partly that of one genre breaking into another: though Mora has cited the Westerns of Sam Peckinpah as inspiration, the degree of gore is closer to George Romero's *Night of the Living Dead* (1968). There is historical warrant for the portrayal of anti-Chinese massacres on the goldfields—but like both Peckinpah and Romero, Mora adds an allegorical level of meaning, consciously alluding to the then-recent atrocities of the Vietnam War.

Morgan races outdoors, still clutching his opium pipe, leaping over obstacles as he makes his way to the creek. On the level of psychological realism, we can assume he will spend the rest of the film suffering from post-traumatic stress disorder, like many Vietnam veterans in both cinema and life.[5] Just as significant, however, are the symbolic meanings suggested by the conjunction of fire and water, which recurs throughout the film, always at moments of transition. Both of these opposed elements are traditionally associated with an underworld: respectively the Christian hell and the river Styx of classical myth.

As this suggests, *Mad Dog* belongs in the tradition Ross Gibson has dubbed the 'purgatorial narrative', where Australia is seen as a realm of punishment for sinners groping toward uncertain redemption, following in the footsteps of Christ who (according to the Apostles' Creed) 'descended into hell'. Of course such descents occur in other mythologies too: one influence on *Mad Dog* often cited by Mora is Jean Cocteau's symbolist film *Orphée* (1950), which treats the myth of Orpheus as an allegory of what Cocteau described as 'the poet's need to go through a series of deaths'.

Either way, Morgan descends. Down he goes, into the creek, absurdly attempting to swim through water that barely reaches his knees, and tearing off his shirt before he reaches the opposite bank. Thus he leaves civilisation, never to return. Somehow, the fire seems to have crossed with him; a close-up of a ring of flame at the centre of a charred log suggests a womb from which new, fevered life may emerge.

Soon after, Morgan undertakes his first robbery, the hold-up at the shepherd's hut. As a criminal he's still an amateur, unable to sustain his menacing pose: much of the scene unfolds in fixed long shot, the seemingly artless framing denying him any power. Skipping past his inevitable arrest, we cut straight to the patrician Judge Barry (Peter Collingwood) pronouncing sentence. 'Down, down to hell and say I sent thee thither', Barry mutters, using an obscure but apt Shakespeare quote to mark Morgan's second symbolic death.[6]

The trip to hell involves another journey over water, to an island fort standing in for the prison hulk where the real-life Morgan was sent. Fire comes straight after, as Smith (Bill Hunter), a twitchy guard with a teardrop tattoo, supervises the branding of his prisoner's palm with the letter 'M' for malefactor. At the moment of impact, Smith trembles orgasmically; worse in a way is his preliminary caressing of

Mora, Hopper and chief rapist Max Fairchild prepare for a prison scene.

Morgan's face and neck, obscenely parodying his victim's need for human connection.

Worse still is to come. Mora eventually cuts away from Morgan's rape by his cellmates, but not till we've seen him stripped and held face down in the darkness as the gang cries out 'New meat!' Few men in cinema get raped, and even fewer male protagonists (within Australian cinema, another possible though ambiguous instance is the hero of the similarly purgatorial *Wake in Fright* [1971]). What the branding does to Morgan's body the rape does to his psyche: each is a violent initiation that bars him from returning to the 'normal', civilised world.

The extent of Morgan's disturbance becomes apparent as he serves his sentence of hard labour, breaking rocks in a quarry; ordered to take a rest, he carries on like an automaton, till a guard brings him back to reality with a thump. Months or years later, he's in an ironbark forest, chopping down a slender tree; briefly,

Hard labour: Morgan serves his sentence.

he pauses and runs his hand lovingly down the trunk, as Smith caressed him earlier. Soon after comes a remarkable tracking shot past numerous prisoners hacking into the trees with axes and saws: another gang rape, of Nature rather than of an individual.

Finally, an outwardly deferential Morgan is given his ticket of leave by his parole officer, who sits at a desk with a shelf of skulls behind him. Implausibly, Morgan recognises one of them as belonging to a gorilla; the officer explains that they will be used by Professor Halford, mentioned here for the first time, in a lecture on 'the relations of man to apes'.

Morgan himself seems to have slipped down the evolutionary ladder, a point spelled out straight after by the film's narrator

Manwaring, once again addressing the camera as he instructs us on the biological basis of criminality: 'Nature requires time to produce her Titans, and these monsters reappear after the lapse of years.' True to the Gothic idiom, a clap of thunder heralds a glimpse of Morgan stealing a horse on a dark and stormy night, sufficiently long after his release for him to have grown his soon-to-be notorious black beard.

Is *Mad Dog* a Western, and if so, of what kind? Critics have proposed comparisons not only to Peckinpah but to so-called spaghetti Westerns like those of Sergio Leone, which by Mora's account were less directly influential. What is undeniable is that the film closely relates to what the critic Jonathan Rosenbaum has dubbed the 'acid Western', in which the tropes of the genre are recreated in anachronistic, psychedelic terms.[7]

This 'acid Western' quality can be felt in a weirdly lyrical shot following Morgan's theft of the horse, as its owner Evan Evans (John Derum) and his friend Bond (Ken Weaver) go in pursuit of the thief. The pair ride along a granite ridge that divides the screen; the hills and low clouds in the distance have the unreality of a matte painting, while rock pools in the foreground reflect the riders and the sky. If Mora's visual style can be described in terms of an alternation between flatness and depth, here these qualities are combined in a single image: a polarised filter makes the characters pop out from their surroundings, like actors isolated on the stage of history.

This sets the scene for the reappearance of Morgan, viewed for the first time through another character's eyes: seated on his stolen horse atop the ridge, bearded and ominous, wind whistling around him. Bond fires, and suddenly the camera is close to the ground, frantically following a trail of blood. The gunshot has laid Morgan low, in a third symbolic death: he's vanished into the wind, into thin air. Or as Evans puts it, looking around bewildered: 'Disappears like a bloody black!'

Cue the didgeridoo. A close-up of a spotted snake slithering over bloodstained ground evokes—as the scholar Helene Forscher has observed—the graphic patterns of Indigenous art. And here comes Gulpilil's Billy, stealing round from behind some rocks in grubby apricot pants that accentuate his graceful bandy-legged walk. 'Take me in your arms, Holy Mother', the wounded Morgan murmurs. Billy clasps Morgan's bloodied hand in immediate friendship; when he locks eyes with Morgan a little later, his grin dazzles like a second sun.

At this point, *Mad Dog* is close to Jim Jarmusch's *Dead Man* (1995), the film Rosenbaum sees as the culmination of the 'acid Western' tradition: both centre on a bumbling white protagonist who is almost killed in a shootout before recreating himself with help from a 'native' guide. In each case, the escape from civilisation implies an escape from adulthood, enabling the formation of a homoerotic yet innocent bond: Billy's killing of the spotted snake—cracking it like a whip, then crushing its head—suggests the expulsion of phallic sexuality from his and Morgan's Eden. Once again, a transition between states is signalled by imagery of fire and water; but both forces are at their most benign, represented by the barbecuing of the snake and by a shot of Billy bathing in a waterfall that evokes both 'natural' sensuality and cleansing baptism.

'What was Billy's tribe?' Gulpilil wonders today. Clearly Mora did not know enough to give an answer; Billy remains an abstractly conceived character, not far removed from the stereotype of the

'Take me in your arms': Billy (David Gulpilil) tends to the wounded Morgan. (Photo: Angus Forbes)

noble savage. Yet his role in the narrative is a complex one. He's a double for Morgan, a shadow self (one of the real Morgan's aliases was 'Billy the Native'). He's also, as Morgan indicates, a mother or carer, lovingly tending to his injured charge; the pair find refuge in a womblike mountain cave, where Morgan slips back towards infancy just as the land seems to return to a time before white invasion.

Most vitally, Billy is a teacher: not only does he show Morgan how to throw a spear and a boomerang, he educates him politically, casually referring to whites coming to kill his tribe. *Mad Dog* thus

Shadow, mother and teacher: David Gulpilil as Billy. (Photo: Angus Forbes)

becomes one of the very few films from this period or earlier to acknowledge the historical reality of genocide in Australia—which haunts the entire film, as Rosenbaum says of the equivalent Native American genocide in *Dead Man*, 'without ever quite taking centre stage'. Billy's motive for teaming with Morgan is at least partly revenge: like the Native American character played by Gary Farmer in *Dead Man*, he encourages his friend to adopt a new identity that will centrally involve terrorising and killing other white men.

Morgan is now ready to return to bushranging, but in a newly self-conscious way: he must *imagine* himself as a bushranger, adopt the role. Standing in front of rocks like those where Billy first found him, he points two guns at the camera and demands: 'Your money or your life!' The scene recalls the bandit firing at the camera in the early Western *The Great Train Robbery* (1903), one of the first moments of overt reflexivity in cinema; just as Morgan himself has been born again, the film performs the archetypal modernist gesture of returning to the 'primitive' past in order to make it new.

This 'primitivism' means that fiction and documentary become indistinguishable: after an extended sequence of Billy (or Gulpilil) dancing, we're given some equally candid glimpses of Morgan (or Hopper) improvising different versions of the 'money or your life' routine, intercut with a growing pile of loot. Within the fiction, Morgan is presumably carrying out a series of actual robberies— but these are represented in a blatantly anti-illusionistic manner, Hopper going through the motions like a child at play.

Morgan has survived his ordeals, and come out the other side. Or has he? Despite Billy's healing love, he remains conscious of an absence in himself—which he seeks to fill with a new identity,

'I could look like this man Lincoln': Morgan plans a makeover. (Photo: Angus Forbes for the Australian Information Service. Courtesy National Library of Australia)

shaving his moustache so he can look like a newspaper portrait of Abraham Lincoln. According to Mora, the scene was devised at the last moment, mainly to justify modifications to Hopper's unconvincing false beard. Still, it suggests that Morgan shares desires with many a self-estranged anti-hero of modern cinema: to cut a figure in the eyes of the world, and to align himself with an existing 'star'. The truth is that Morgan is not Lincoln, nor Jesus; he is not even Ned Kelly, the Australian answer to both. At most, he is Kelly's John the Baptist: a voice crying in the wilderness, a prefiguration. He has no band of disciples, no gospel of his own. But he has Billy.

VI. Morgan at Bay

The central half hour of *Mad Dog* is the most unhinged, the closest to Morgan's own paranoia. Causality slackens: there is no necessary connection between things, between one scene and the next. Gaps open up, the wind blows between them. Shead compares the landscape—flat horizons, or hills obscuring whatever lies beyond—not just to Nolan but to Dali and Max Ernst: 'The only structures are flimsy, hardly there at all.' Rarely do we know where one location sits in relation to another, despite the illegible maps tacked up on walls in interior scenes. Nor do we know how much time has passed: half-forgotten characters may reappear at any moment unaltered. Morgan himself metamorphoses but does not age: he sits outside not just civilisation but the Western notion of progress, his cave a base from which he mounts guerrilla raids on history.

This does not mean he knows what he is doing. The best account of his situation comes from Mora himself in a *Cinema Papers* article analysing the role of Buster Keaton in *Cops* (1922): 'Buster does not seem to have any free will. He is in a world out of his control. Something is always happening, but he does not have much time to think because events always keep ahead of him.' The film becomes a surreal chase comedy, with Morgan darting about like a hunted animal or a refugee; fortunately his pursuers are even more lost than he is, fixated on signs and traces which seem to mark out a path but are equally likely to lead them astray.

These opponents have names, titles, claims to importance, but all this recedes into the film's dim background, while the foreground is occupied by what critics for the last few decades have been calling 'the materiality of the signifier'. Listen to the way Baylis (John Hargreaves), one of Morgan's first hold-up victims, gabbles his outrage in a 'refined' British accent: 'Shot be damned, I'm the magistrate of Wagga Wagga.' Morgan makes an Irish mockery of this, drawing out the vowels: 'Ah, it's Mr *Wagga Wagga*, is it? Oh, well… ' After an exchange of threats, the scene concludes with Morgan relishing the syllables in 'boomerang' while Billy, who used an actual boomerang to knock Baylis off his horse, imitates a kookaburra.

This launches a round-robin tournament pitting Hopper's Morgan against one Aussie acting icon after another. Baylis goes after Morgan with some troopers, leading to a chaotic, nearly incomprehensible night-time shootout, where Baylis wounds Billy in the arm and Billy in turn wounds Baylis, who's also struck by an accidental bullet from one of his own men. After this Baylis disappears for a while, and his place is taken by Bill Hunter's Smith—who has risen from sadistic jailer to sadistic police sergeant, while remaining unaware that the elusive Morgan is his former prisoner.

Meanwhile, Morgan himself rises to fame, abetted by the good-natured French photographer Roget (Robin Ramsay), an invented character Shead not unreasonably sees as Mora's own representative on screen. Given a hero's welcome at a pub, Morgan finally appears to have found a place in society, though the

On the warpath: Bill Hunter as Sergeant Smith.

mood briefly sours when he's forced to defend Billy from a racist drunk. After draining his glass—the first alcohol we've seen him consume—Morgan makes his exit amid backslapping and ribald joking: 'He's got giant balls, that one', the publican says, shoving a couple of potatoes down his pants to show his meaning.

Morgan, man of the people, but only to a point. An attempt to play Robin Hood, forcing the squatter Gibson (Peter Cummins) to write cheques for his employees, is not quite the moment of glory he might have planned. His verbal abuse of Gibson has a desperate obscenity we have not heard from him before; when one of his beneficiaries describes him as 'bloodthirsty' he takes offence, snatching the proffered cheque back from the ingrate. This is also the moment he chooses to stage his own version of the attack on the opium den: Billy sets a barn alight with a stick then gallops about joyously, while men flee, sheep scatter, and Morgan chants obsessively 'Burn it down!'

A similar need to repeat past trauma is evident in the trick Morgan plays on Haley (David Mitchell), a shepherd he suspects of being an informer. A bucket of offal sits near Haley's hut; remembering his long-ago clash with Wendlan on the goldfields, Morgan dumps the guts over the unconscious Haley, who, on waking, believes himself to be hideously wounded. For once, Mora might be accused of altering the facts to make his hero more sympathetic: in reality Haley *was* shot by Morgan, although not fatally. But the Morgan of the film is not yet a killer, and seems to have devised an allegory of his own rather than carry out a literal bloody revenge.

To drive home the point, Mora provides Morgan with an allegorical stand-in: a black dog that gobbles up the guts, perhaps the same black dog present during the confrontation with Wendlan. This suggests how Morgan's becoming-legend, projecting an image separate from himself, is bound up with his becoming-animal: if society insists on labelling him as a beast, his only viable course is to accept this identity, which can be drawn on as a source of power. Man (and woman) as beast is a theme that recurs in many of Mora's later movies, including his two sequels to Joe Dante's werewolf film *The Howling* (1981); Billy comes close to identifying Morgan as a 'wolf-man' when he presents his friend with the skin of a thylacine, a creature more canine than feline despite its alternate name of 'Tasmanian tiger'.[8]

The deeper meaning of this totemic identity emerges when Morgan and Billy show up at the Round Hill station to keep an appointment with the absent Roget. Exuding an avuncular authority unlike any character we've met so far, the station manager Watson (Philip Ross) invites Morgan, though not Billy, in for a glass of rum. Conveniently, a picture of a thylacine hangs in the sitting room: 'That's an extinct animal, Morgan', Watson explains, 'like you'. Morgan, then, is not just a beast but a doomed one—a judgment that confirms his status as a proxy for Australia's Indigenous peoples, long viewed as less than human and destined to die out.

Suddenly, everything comes together and falls apart. Blind drunk on Watson's rum, Morgan emerges from the house and tries unsuccessfully to clamber onto his horse. Watson follows him, also drunk, his authority all gone. A gale is blowing, though only on one side of the screen. Morgan succeeds in pulling himself up into the saddle, before realising in fury that Watson is mocking him; he fires into the gale, a warning shot. Somehow, the bullet ricochets, hitting Watson in the hand and Heriot (Bruce Spence), one of the station hands, in the leg. For the moment, nobody grasps what has happened: logic and meaning are out of their proper places, swept up like leaves in the wind.

A shaken Morgan orders another station hand, the stuttering McLean (David Bracks), to ride off and fetch a doctor for Heriot. Straight after, Billy, who has observed all this impassively, warns that McLean will instead go for the police. Morgan accepts Billy's warning without question, taking off like a dog set on a foe; no longer shrinking from bloodshed, he rides after McLean, spies him in a field of Paterson's Curse and shoots him down. An overhead shot of the dying McLean on his back recalls a similar inverted figure in one of Nolan's best-known Kelly paintings, *Death of Constable Scanlon*: the images share a faux-naïf flatness, setting us at a distance that adds to the horror.

This killing is soon followed by another, the panicked Morgan firing instinctively when he encounters one Sergeant Maginnity (Grant Page, here doubling as actor as well as stuntman) in a bush clearing. The resulting guilt radically threatens the identity Morgan has snatched from the brink of total psychological collapse—and so he all but disappears from his own film, as we follow the unlovely Smith on the trail of Maginnity's killer. This mini-saga culminates in a third murder, Morgan rematerialising just in time to shoot Smith at point-blank range, while magically coloured light glints off a lake at sunset. 'You!' gasps Smith just before he's shot, as he grants the recognition Morgan craves above all things—recognition as an old acquaintance but also, perhaps, as a messenger of death itself.

By now we might well view Morgan as some kind of monster; what we're never allowed to forget is that worse monsters surround him. Smith's body has hardly hit the ground when another nemesis springs up: Frank Thring's obscenely pompous Superintendent Cobham, the film's ultimate authority figure and from this point onward one of its central presences.

Cobham is not a double of Morgan. Rather, the two complement each other: where Morgan is a hysterical body at loose in the landscape, Cobham is almost immobile behind his desk, framed by stuffed marsupials that suggest a grisly coat of arms. Though the pair never exactly meet face-to-face, their relationship is an archetypal one: that of Prospero to Caliban, Frankenstein

The ultimate authority figure: Frank Thring as Superintendent Cobham.

to his creation, or Dr Moreau to the beast-men on his island of lost souls. In short, the qualities Cobham denounces in Morgan are those he refuses to recognise in himself: while his imposing bald head identifies him as a representative of intellect, no head was ever so visibly part of a body, so grossly physical and bestial. Wittily, Mora makes the point by dollying in first on Cobham as he warns of the consequences should Morgan cross from New South Wales into Victoria—and then on one of Cobham's pet pit bulls, which stares down the camera with equal menace.

Truth be told, Cobham's intellect is a slow one: it takes some time to get an idea through that great meaty head. Chatting over lunch with his friend Dr Dobbyn (Kurt Beimel, the actor who had to be poked) he nods thoughtfully but not quite comprehendingly as Dobbyn refers to Professor Halford and speculates that Morgan may be part-gorilla. As Mora has observed, this garbled Darwinism foreshadows the eugenics theories of the Nazis; more overtly, it suggests that the colonial Establishment is as mad as Morgan, not least in its unquestioning faith in science and reason.

As this central section of the film concludes, Morgan—who has regrown his moustache—decides that he and Billy will head for Victoria despite Cobham's warning. To mark their departure, they bathe one last time in the waterfall, an intimate moment Mora chooses not to show onscreen. Sitting with Billy on the bank afterwards, Morgan proposes that in Victoria they part ways: Billy will head for Wangaratta to keep an eye on the police, while Morgan settles some 'old scores'. The plan implies they'll meet again, but the words are empty; he knows as well as we do that the crossing means death.

VII. Morgan's Country

Over the border, Morgan moves more than ever within his own dream: his legend precedes him, so wherever he travels becomes 'Morgan's country'. Having crossed the river, he seems compelled to continue the association of water and fire: we see him stealing up on some haystacks and setting them alight, waking a youth dozing on a bench who sounds the alarm, all of this in one shaky but impressive tracking shot.

Morgan is in disarray as he stands by the fire, bailing up John Evans (David John) and a group of servants. At first his rage is genuinely frightening, but it recedes quickly when he's informed of the absence of John's brother Evan Evans, whom he holds partly responsible for his being shot. Robbed of his planned revenge for that injury, Morgan starts to ramble like a has-been stage performer trying to engage the crowd: 'You're a bloody cheerful-looking lot. Has anyone seen my waxwork in the museum?' This waxwork is his externalised self-image in solid form: another of his doubles, as well as a preview of his corpse.[9]

A close-up of the burning hay renews the association between fire and sexuality, the crinkling strands resembling pubic hair: this shot leads into a comic outburst from a young servant woman clearly aroused by the departing Morgan or rather by the aura of his celebrity. 'The way he looked at me, undressing me with his eyes… Horrible. Disgusting.' The unexpected notion of Morgan as sex object recurs in the next major scene, where he enters a dingy-looking inn, a pointed contrast to the earlier crowded pub in New South Wales. Mora shoots the bar with a characteristic wide-angle lens, an empty bottle in the foreground giving almost the effect of 3D. An old woman sits in a darkened corner, with no other customers present. The barmaid is young and attractive, in a low-cut, loose-fitting white dress: her confidently welcoming posture conveys both open sexuality and a hint of the maternal.

In the midst of this we cut to Manwaring—now upgraded from narrator to fully fledged character—and his overseer Superintendent Winch (Michael Pate). Scrutinising a map in an office somewhere, the pair act as proxies for the audience, straining to decipher the logic of Morgan's erratic movements. In what is nominally a 'straight man' role, Thompson gives a markedly eccentric performance, grasping a riding crop and lingering on his lines in a manner that suggests a lascivious zest for the hunt.

Back to the inn, where the barmaid has joined Morgan at his table. A fire crackles behind her. Struggling to meet her gaze, he holds up a finger and tries a joke about her skimpy clothing: 'I think you're probably feeling a wind.' Abruptly, she bares her breasts. Looking on like one of the Fates, the old woman grins, squints and hides her face in mock-defence against obscene knowledge. Morgan quotes a snatch of Irish poetry. The old woman snickers. Gently, in bewilderment and regret, Morgan apologises for his inability to perform as required, repeating a line about being a 'tired stranger'. The barmaid rejoins that he's no stranger, identifying him as Daniel Morgan. Somehow, the name breaks the spell. He finishes his drink, gives thanks and leaves; thoughtfully the barmaid buttons up her dress.

This is unusual behaviour for a hero, although Mora defended the scene at the time in terms of realism: 'People just don't go leaping on to women at every opportunity.' The key to a deeper interpretation lies in the verse recited by Morgan, in fact the second half of W.B. Yeats' epigram 'A Stick of Incense', which is worth citing in full:

'You're no stranger': Liza Lee-Atkinson as the barmaid.

> Whence did all that fury come?
> From empty tomb or Virgin womb?
> St Joseph thought the world would melt
> But liked the way his finger smelt.

The recitation was of course improvised by Hopper, who liked to memorise verse and work it into his dialogue; Mora says he had no idea of the source of the poem, written some seventy years after the period in which the film is set. But meaning can exist in films regardless of anyone's intent, and it is worth examining what the words imply. Yeats, no friend to organised religion, pits its empty promise of transcendence against a physical fullness evoked through an obscene joke about the sex life of the mother of Christ. Morgan, however, seems to conflate the sexual and the spiritual, responding to the barmaid's body with a kind of sacred horror.

Morgan tells the barmaid that he learned the verse at St Mary's in Sydney, a real school though not one the real Morgan seems likely to have attended; he then excuses his inadequacies as a lover by referring to a second Mary, his own mother, as the only woman he ever knew. In conflating his mother with the Virgin, and both with women generally, Morgan indicates that for him heterosexuality, taking the place of the Father, is taboo as both blasphemy and incest: thus he identifies himself both with St Joseph—traditionally imagined as impotent—and with the equally asexual Christ.

There is yet another layer here. According to the poet and scholar John Hollander, the poem is built on a traditional analogy between two St Josephs: Christ's foster-father, and St Joseph of Arimathea, who took Christ's body from the cross and laid it in the tomb. Thus Yeats' title refers both to the suggestively smelly finger of the first Joseph, and to literal incense used in the burial process by the second. By this reckoning, Morgan is simultaneously looking back to the circumstances of his birth and forward to the fate of his corpse, suggesting a cyclical view of history already implicit in the act of quoting words not yet written.

Much of this will be echoed and amplified in the dream sequence to come. But there's ground to be covered first, including

Detective Manwaring (Jack Thompson) loses patience with the men.

one last bail-up: the victim, 'Italian Jack', is played by none other than Graeme Blundell, well-known at the time from the hit local sex comedy *Alvin Purple* (1973), whose appearance at this juncture registers as an intertextual joke about the tendency of Australian film heroes to shrink from women. Morgan has fallen a long way since his defence of the Chinese miner: he treats this petrified outsider with genial contempt, looming over him on horseback and tossing him a pound note while warning that 'I may have to take it back from yer someday'. Unusually, he declines the offer of a drink. Meanwhile, Manwaring, hot on Morgan's trail, grows irritated with troopers who pose witless questions about where their quarry might be headed: 'Morgan is bound for hell!'

'Allegories are, in the realm of thoughts, what ruins are in the realm of things', wrote Walter Benjamin. As his end nears, Morgan seems to gravitate to such ruins, burnt-out locations which retain only traces of meaning. Sheltering at sunset in a deserted woolshed, he meets a friendly old swagman who speaks innocently of how Morgan the bold bushranger has put the fear of God into the landowners of New South Wales, 'so they're frightened to refuse a man a feed'. As with the offscreen waxwork, Morgan encounters his own legend, this time in the form of a reassuring bedtime story. The wind whistles past the campfire as he and the swagman turn in for the night.

Then comes the dream, a direct tribute to Cocteau: the plunging water, the mad eyes, the burning man rising to the top of the cliff where he encounters Morgan and leaps upon him. There is no single, definitive way to interpret this sequence, which, as we've seen, Mora and Grant Page went to enormous lengths to shoot. An early draft of the *Mad Dog* script suggests the burning man was originally the vengeful ghost of Page's character Sergeant Maginnity, slain by Morgan long before. But while close examination of the footage confirms that Page is still in his trooper's uniform, it is unlikely that any viewer would spontaneously make the connection, especially as we never get a clear look at the burning man's face. Even Mora nowadays hedges his bets, at most allowing that what he meant to symbolise was Morgan's 'doom coming at him'.

Extrapolating from this, it might be said that the burning man represents the monstrous projected image which Morgan has brought into being, and which by now has grown more powerful than its creator. This can be understood as an allegory of the artist who 'dies' in the creation of the work he hopes will outlast him: a pool is also a mirror, and so the reflection of Morgan that emerges from the depths suggests not only Orpheus, the artist figure in Cocteau's work, but also Narcissus. Colliding with his transfigured double, Morgan is like a time traveller crossing his own path—again implying that events move in a cycle, and that the successive 'deaths' he has experienced prefigure his impending fate.

On a separate level, the dream marks the culmination of the film's pattern of sexual imagery, with an Edenic sensuality associated with Billy—evoked through the waterfall and the accompanying didgeridoo—giving way inexorably to full heterosexuality, symbolised by the contrasting energies of water and fire, and thence to the burning man emerging from the waterhole like a child thrust out into a threatening world. On this reading, Morgan appears in the dream three times over: as father, son, and impossible onlooker at his own conception and birth. The horror in his gaze is finally that of recognising the self as material, part of a contingent creation—a perception magnified by the successive traumas he's suffered, culminating in the rape that reduced him to mere thingness or 'meat'.

Yet another interpretation is possible. The sequence emulates Cocteau's intentionally 'primitive' special effects, such as the use of reverse motion to enable the fragments of a shattered mirror to fly back together; for Cocteau, this device alludes to cinema's own ability to defy time and resurrect the dead, and it is not unreasonable to think it carries that meaning for Mora as well (we might remember Mirka and her family retreating to safety from the Nazi camp, like figures on a strip of film being wound back). Of course, there's a catch: the trickery calls attention to the artifice of the medium, becoming one more alienation effect. What we're offered is transparent falsehood, the precise opposite of what we know really happened—which amounts to an admission of the false promise of the movies, perhaps of all art.

Morgan wakes, to find the fire still burning. 'You're Morgan, aren't you?' says the swagman, offering the same ritual recognition as the barmaid earlier. Morgan does not deny it, and the swagman asks why his companion has come to Victoria, where swarms of police are on the hunt. Morgan's voice quavers, as if he were pleading for understanding: 'My God, man, for revenge.'

Meanwhile Billy has been arrested and brought to Cobham, who sits at his desk toying with a leash before slowly rising to his feet. 'There's no need to be afraid', he rumbles as he advances on Billy, his full monstrosity plain at last. There's a cliffhanger cut; the film's whole climax will be made sinister by the lack of any reference to Billy's fate.

VIII. Morgan's Last Stand

Macpherson (Wallas Eaton) and his family are in the dining room at Peechelba, listening to one of the daughters of the household play the piano, when there's knocking at the door. Morgan sidles in, clutching his shotgun but introducing himself with odd humility: 'I be Morgan. I suppose you've heard of me.' Apologising for his appearance, he angles for an invitation to dinner; with deep reluctance, Macpherson offers him a seat.

Events play out as we know they must. Alice Keenan (Elsie Wishart) asks to slip away to the nursery. Morgan consents, waving his hand like a fine gentleman, before returning to his menacing persona: 'But if you're too long, you'll be the one that's sick.' He then insists on hearing the piano, which he refers to as an organ, presumably recalling his churchgoing childhood. The melody is the parlour ballad 'I Dreamt That I Dwelt in Marble Halls'—apt both to Morgan's dreams of glory as a bushranger, and his sudden envy of the Macphersons' genteel family life.

Morgan, as he listens, is seen in frontal close-up, the world lost in shadow aside from a flickering candle above the piano and the hazy profile of the Macpherson daughter as she plays. In between his black hat and his black beard, what we see of his face is dominated by mad staring eyes, so that he seems nearly as extreme a figure as Kelly painted by Nolan: scarcely human,

Dreams of glory: Morgan approaching death.

yet painfully so. Breathing heavily and close to tears, he launches into a murmured monologue, typically incoherent but with its own stumbling music:

> Mr Macpherson, I've missed so much of my life, sir. I've missed so much of my life, sir. And I'm not trying to be sentimental either, I'm not trying to be. Do you know how lucky I am to be Dan Morgan, sir? Do you know how lucky I am to be Dan Morgan, sir? I… I could have… well, you only go around once, as they say. I tell you what, that Irish whisky's pretty good.

Pure Method in approach, the speech—quoted here only in part— sums up the paradox of a performer consciously striving to be 'authentic'. In its stammering banality, it threatens to collapse into an unmediated cry of pain, and yet Morgan remains intensely conscious of putting on an act, wishing to appear in a certain light ('I'm not trying to be sentimental').

While Hopper is let off the leash as an actor, Mora's style here is at its most classically expressive, precisely defining the film's double view of Morgan. While the music lasts, the sustained close-up draws us into his sorrow, his longing for the delicacy of which he is supposedly incapable; then a wide shot jolts us back to the perspective of his prisoners, frozen in horror and far from comprehending their captor's grotesque pity for himself. Hopper, improvising once again, had clearly taken the eyewitness accounts of the evening into his soul: in its black comedy and its pathos without special pleading, it is one of the most memorable scenes in all Australian cinema.

Two armed groups are now on their way: one led by Manwaring, and the other summoned by Rutherford (Gerard Maguire), the station co-owner who lives nearby. Meanwhile, Morgan continues to rave drunkenly, alternating between fury and regret; in a somewhat strained touch, we see him wiping away tears, facing the camera so as to conceal this from everyone but the viewer. Sitting up and drinking with Macpherson, he taunts his Scottish host, mockingly singing 'Rule Britannia' and cursing her Majesty's police. A moment later, he reaches out and strokes Macpherson's sleeve—trying, once again, to make a friend.

As dawn breaks, Mora's characteristic tracking shots reveal the forces gathered around the Macphersons' home. The colours are glaringly bright, the action not always fully legible: the men are often half-hidden behind trees and bushes, or in deep shadow.

Manwaring arrives and attempts to assume command, baring his teeth in low-angle close-up as he insists that Morgan be taken alive. One of the armed civilians turns out to be none other than Wendlan, Morgan's first enemy, and thus the film comes full circle (though not all viewers will instantly recall Morgan's encounter with Wendlan on the goldfields, a scene which in any case is wholly fictional).

Morgan, sitting at the breakfast table, is quite conscious of what awaits him: he has a zombie look, as if his death were an accomplished fact. He asks that his thylacine skin be fetched, acknowledging the truth of the prophecy that he too will soon go extinct. As he prepares to step outside he wraps himself in the skin, a last stage in becoming-animal (which is also becoming-Indigenous, in the sense of accepting the identity bestowed by Billy; as Helene Forscher says, the sequence 'resonates with references to Aboriginal ceremony'). Emerging from the house, he appears to have arrived at a sense of peace indistinguishable from insanity; rather than looking round for his foes, he gazes upward, murmuring about the need to 'keep smiling'. It's a beautiful day, he keeps saying, and so it is: birds sing out, clouds float in a bright blue sky.

Then Wendlan fires. For a long moment Morgan stays upright, clutching his neck; just before he drops, the camera is pointed straight at the sun, its bleeding light a visual equivalent of the aural shock of the gunshot. Manwaring and others rush towards his prone body on the grass, now filmed from directly overhead as if seen through the eye of God. The calm is dispelled by a flurry of handheld camerawork, as Manwaring flies into a panic. 'Send for the surgeons! Quick, man!'

So Morgan dies in the darkness of a blacksmith's shop, choking on blood and unable to speak. The soundtrack reprises the faltering piano notes of 'Marble Halls', as if piously hoping he will go to a better place; Morgan continues to gaze blankly upward, as if the whole film had been a dream and he had never left the opium den. When Dobbyn, as coroner, announces that all is over, almost everyone acts appropriately solemn; the exception is Wendlan, who pulls a knife to cut a souvenir lock of Morgan's beard. Manwaring, enraged, duplicates Morgan's behaviour at the start of the film, leaping on Wendlan and wrestling him to the ground.

This last invented bit of business hardly tallies with Manwaring's character, even if the 'animal' qualities conveyed by Thompson suggest a hidden kinship with Morgan. Primarily, the sequence exists to give relief to the viewer—though any sense of catharsis is a qualified one. When Manwaring and Wendlan crash through the wall of the blacksmith's shop, it's a moment of slapstick bathos; and when the horsewhipping administered by Manwaring is witnessed by a group of children, there's a hint of dismay at a cycle of violence set to continue indefinitely.

Back at Beechworth, Manwaring reads a final extract from his manuscript. Only now does it become evident that the entire film has unfolded in flashback—and the film's Brechtian opening is retrospectively naturalised, since Manwaring is revealed to be addressing not the audience but a group of mostly familiar characters, assembled like the survivors at the end of a Shakespearean tragedy. Morgan is laid out on a stretcher, wearing dusty grey clothes and looking much like the images that have come down to us of the real man after his death: the legend fixed and complete at last. Reluctantly, Morgan's former ally Roget takes one last photo of Wendlan holding his rifle over the corpse (in modern terms, this would be Wendlan's Facebook profile shot). Birds tweet in the distance, and the wind whistles once again.

After Roget and others have left, Cobham gives the order to flay off Morgan's beard and remove his scrotum, which 'might make an interesting tobacco pouch'. In return, Dobbyn requests permission for Morgan's skull to be sent to Halford. Cobham graciously grants this boon, much as Thring's Herod supplied Salome with the head of John the Baptist in *King of Kings*. 'And

Wendlan (Martin Harris) poses with his kill.

don't forget the scrotum.' He strolls away, disappearing round a corner.

Whatever the truth of the scrotum story, it carries the denial of Morgan's humanity to a grimly logical conclusion: not only is he dishonoured after death, but made into an object in the most literal sense. The scene can also be understood as yet another allusion to the Nazis, evoking the story of lampshades and similar household items being made from the skin of Holocaust victims—itself, nowadays, a subject of some historical dispute.

Five brief shots follow, a kind of coda. First comes an almost neutral image of clouds, an echo of Morgan's vision just before his death. In the second shot, these clouds form part of a landscape as tranquil as one of Gill's prints, dark scrub in the foreground giving way to grasslands and then to blue hills that melt into the sky: earth and heaven held in balance, as parts of a whole. Over this we hear what seems to be the laugh of a kookaburra, till the third shot reveals the call is being made by Billy, alive and well and returned to the bush. After a moment he raises his hand, and we see he's holding a shotgun. The image might be captioned with the title of an early Straub-Huillet film, *Not Reconciled* (1965): like Manwaring's outburst, it suggests that Morgan's career represents a single skirmish in a war far from over.

Billy's call echoes over a reprise of the preceding landscape shot, followed by whistling wind over Roget's photograph of the dead Morgan, 'printing the legend' while conveying an irony like the end of *Citizen Kane* (1941): how can a single image explain a man's life? As the credits roll, we hear the folklorist Danny Spooner singing a traditional ballad about Morgan: 'Shot like a dog in the bright early morning/Shot without mercy who mercy had none… ' In context, the moralising words are charged with a related irony, acknowledging that the film we have just seen represents one possible interpretation of the evidence among many.

IX. Morgan's Legacy

Mora likes to tell the story of how he first showed *Mad Dog* to the horrified head of the newly formed Australian Film Commission, who observed that the rape scene was unlikely to increase tourism. Mora rejoined that, on the contrary, he thought it would. What he meant by this is hard to say, but perhaps there was some official relief when *Mad Dog* was well-received at the Cannes Film Festival marketplace, *Variety* declaring Hopper's performance a 'tour de force'. The film won the John Ford Trophy at Cannes' First International Festival of Westerns—an unofficial satellite of the main event—and achieved a more important milestone in becoming one of the first Australian films to be bought by an American distributor.

Most Australian reviewers were impressed, especially by Hopper's acting and Molloy's cinematography. But there was nothing like the audience response that had greeted Peter Weir's more respectably middlebrow *Picnic at Hanging Rock* (1975). In the United States and later the United Kingdom, it was the same story: critical enthusiasm (though the New York papers were sniffy) and modest box office. At the Australian Film Institute awards the following year, there were a couple of nominations but no wins. And that was that. By the end of the '70s *Mad Dog* had all but disappeared from view, attracting little attention locally or internationally for many years.

The filmmakers went their separate ways. Thomas returned to England where he continued what would become a distinguished producing career, teaming with the exiled Polish director Jerzy Skolimowski for *The Shout* (1978) and bringing Molloy along as cinematographer. After a couple of Australian projects came to nothing, Mora was able to use *Mad Dog* as a calling card in Hollywood, signing with United Artists to direct the horror film *The Beast Within* (1982), with the *Howling* sequels just round the corner.

Hopper, of course, was long gone. The praise for *Mad Dog* in Cannes helped revive his reputation as an actor; he took to circling the world like the Flying Dutchman, going from one set to the next. By September 1976, he was headed for the Philippine jungle and Francis Ford Coppola's *Apocalypse Now*, already six months into a shoot that would last well over a year: madness on a scale that Mora could only dream of.

Yet Hopper had not altogether left Morgan behind, bringing a similar blend of puppyish enthusiasm and wolfish aggression to his *Apocalypse* role as the nameless sidekick of the renegade Colonel Kurtz, played by Marlon Brando, James Dean's old hero. At one point Kurtz refers to Hopper's character as a 'mutt'— echoing an off-camera comment made by Brando, whose disgust with Hopper's antics was such that Coppola was forced to prevent the pair coming face-to-face. Bowing to superior authority, Hopper went along with this, finding a follower of his own in the 15-year-old Laurence Fishburne, who had lied about his age to win a supporting role. 'He didn't pay much attention to me, but I shadowed him for a while', Fishburne remembered. 'I thought, "Here's a guy who's really free, here's a guy who's really free".'

All of the protagonists of this story could be described as *marginal* men, who in different ways and to differing degrees have been considered mad, bad and dangerous to know. Morgan, of course, really was these things—though it seems unfair that he should be remembered solely as a brute, when there is no reason to think him any more violent and ruthless than the revered Ned Kelly. His Achilles heel would seem to be the inarticulacy and inconsistency which barred him from successfully playing the role of the outlaw hero: in other words, the judgement of history has been at least partly an aesthetic one.

Mora too has had rough treatment from his critics, who have too often written him off as if a title like *Howling III—The Marsupials* (1987) indicated naive trash rather than knowing parody. In fact, the distinctive thing about Mora's work is his refusal to play by the rules of either popular or art cinema—a refusal which has undoubtedly hampered his career, and perhaps accounts for his failure to receive any significant funding from the Australian government. Nearly all his work is interesting, even when he is constrained by his budget or producers or both; but many of his most promising projects remain unrealised, and he is not the Antipodean Kubrick or Welles he might once have hoped to become.

Hopper is the trickiest case of all. Back in Hollywood in time for the Reagan era, he gave up liquor and hard drugs, turned Republican, and became a living legend with a string of performances capitalising on his image as a 1960s burnout. From then till his death in 2010, it was a comfortable life of golfing, pursuing his interest in the fine arts, and playing more character roles, usually villains. He even directed a few more films, though none as audacious as those from the first half of his career.

It sounds like a happy ending, or near enough. But late in life, Hopper himself had doubts: 'I never played the great part. I never felt that I directed the great movie. And I can't say it's anybody's fault but my own.' There's no consensus on how much he finally achieved as either actor or director—and even his latter-day image as a reformed citizen was somewhat tarnished by his 1999 arrest for marijuana possession, not to mention his blasé 2004 comments on his record of violence towards women ('I wasn't handcuffing them and beating them to death or anything'). Was Hopper a monster, a buffoon, a visionary? Still today, he resists pigeonholing, though there's no doubt that he could behave like all three.

Mad Dog itself looks in hindsight like a quintessential 'cult' film, and it's no mystery why commercial success never eventuated—or why it fell off the critical radar, even aside from video copies being poor quality and hard to come by. For one thing, it does not fit the accepted narrative that divides Australian cinema of the revival period into commercial genre exercises and worthy period pieces. *Mad Dog* was both of these or neither, blending unabashed sensationalism with genuine curiosity about Australian history, while drawing on modernist sources with little currency in Australian culture then or now.

There is a further sense in which *Mad Dog* stands apart from the mainstream of the Australian film revival, a movement preoccupied to the point of obsession with the problem of how to show a young nation coming to adulthood. A preliminary answer was offered by *Wake in Fright*, in which the naive schoolteacher hero is initiated into Australian culture through a series of gruelling rituals including a bloody animal sacrifice in the form of a kangaroo hunt. Comparable sacrifices are portrayed, with varying degrees of irony, in many subsequent films of the revival era—a pattern culminating in Peter Weir's *Gallipoli* (1981), in which the wartime death of the innocent grazier's son Archy (Mark Lee) atones for the sins of the British ruling class, mythically fusing white Australians into a single people.

As filmmakers, Mora and Weir have much in common, including a willingness to breach genre boundaries as well as an abiding interest in the 'primitive'. Yet Mora's vision of the birth of Australian society—allegory, not myth—differs radically from Weir's. The Morgan of *Mad Dog* remains an unresolvably ambiguous figure: neither innocent nor wholly guilty, both brutal killer and victim. Thus his death cannot be understood in terms of healing, unifying ritual; rather, it allows the colonial authorities to transfer their 'animal' qualities onto him, while continuing to oppress those below.

Given the abuse heaped on the real Morgan by journalists and historians from his day to ours, there is something naggingly plausible about the suggestion that he has functioned as a scapegoat. Not only *Mad Dog* but many of Mora's other films critique this kind of scapegoating—a position summed up, with unexpected lucidity, in his no-budget mockumentary *The Gertrude Stein Mystery or Some Like It Art* (2010). Midway through this bizarre production (which consists largely of the director cavorting in drag) the novelist D.M. Thomas suggests that the Nazis demonised the Jews to avoid facing their own darkness: 'If you can deal with your demons honestly, you don't have to have a projected figure.'

As we've seen in the case of Morgan, the demonisation of such 'projected figures' tends to be rationalised in terms that are aesthetic as much as moral: thus something like an ethical stance is implicit in Mora's own refusal to separate high art from low. Here it's impossible to improve on the words of Bill Routt, the critic who has written best about badness in Australian cinema. Routt's essay on the Australian silent classic *The Sentimental Bloke* (1919) brilliantly rethinks the familiar concept of the 'cultural cringe', observing that when a human or animal cringes (like a dog)

> it is re-enacting an overdetermined, negative and outcast vision of ourselves: it is becoming-scapegoat. Figuratively, a cringing thing takes on all the sins of the world. It sacrifices its objective worthiness so that you or I or Them may be subjectively worthy, which is surely the noblest deed that can be imagined.

But cringing can also be a form of resistance, if a necessarily ironic one. Routt implies as much in another of his essays, which identifies a strategic badness as a persistent quality of Australian cultural artifacts: not merely the artful primitivism of Nolan's Kelly paintings, but a mundanely recognisable abjection born from mingled defiance and self-loathing, 'the badness of a *refusal* to make good'.

In one of the few overall critical assessments of Mora's body of work, Philip Brophy writes admiringly of a 'flair for the perverse... even if it be to the detriment of the finished film'. Another way to put this is to say that Mora's films are often characterised by a badness which the director seems willingly to take upon himself, as Morgan accepts the identity conferred by his 'malefactor' brand. This badness, in *Mad Dog*, is of a kind which every viewer can recognise: in Hopper's raving and flailing, in cheap costumes and phony beards, in lurid violence and gratuitous nudity, in awkward framing and abrupt cuts. Like Morgan in his day, the filmmakers are entangled in this badness, complicit, unable or unwilling to separate themselves. So is 'Australian cinema'—and, as viewers, so are we.

X. Morgan Restored

As the twenty-first century approached, the critical tide on *Mad Dog* was starting to turn. Tom O'Regan, in his book *Australian National Cinema* (1996) and Brian McFarlane, in the *Oxford Companion to Australian Film* (1999) both offered brief but sympathetic treatments. In early 2003 the film was given pride of place in a retrospective of bushranger films at Melbourne's newly-opened Australian Centre for the Moving Image; then, in 2009, came Umbrella Entertainment's DVD release of an uncut, restored version in anamorphic widescreen with commentary by Mora, allowing home viewers to experience the film in a manner not too far from its makers' intentions.[10]

The key event in all this was *Mad Dog*'s inclusion in Mark Hartley's iconoclastic 2008 documentary *Not Quite Hollywood: The Wild, Untold Story of Ozploitation!*, which by now must have reached a wider public than any other history of Australian cinema. Hartley accepted the conventional wisdom dividing revival films into quality middlebrow production on the one hand and 'mid-Pacific' hackwork on the other; but rather than prestige directors like Weir, he championed the likes of John D. Lamond, Brian Trenchard-Smith and Richard Franklin, specialists in skin flicks, stunts and Gothic horror. His enthusiasm was backed by that of his key interview subject, celebrity super-fan Quentin Tarantino—who had first encountered what he called

'Aussieploitation' in the United States drive-ins and fleapits of the late 1970s and early 1980s, and who possessed the advantage of having no stake whatever in Australian culture wars.

Something should be said about the word 'Ozploitation', Hartley's adaptation of Tarantino's coinage. Hartley himself maintains that he simply needed a buzzword meaning Australian genre filmmaking of the revival era—but words, like films, have a life of their own, and the gesture of superimposing 'Aussie' on 'exploitation' is unavoidably heavy with significance. Strictly speaking, 'exploitation' does not designate a genre at all, but rather the use of genre as a pretext for the showcasing of some marketable attraction: sex, violence, grotesquery, but also novelty of any kind, in form as well as content. Thus what dedicated exploitation fans tend to cherish is not ritual or formula but its surrealist reverse: those excessive moments when, as Tarantino puts it in *Not Quite Hollywood*, 'you can't believe you're seeing what you're seeing'.

In essence, this aesthetic is one that views exploitation films as good *because* of their badness: their crudity and aggression, their lack of conscious art. This badness may be valued because, as Carol Laseur argues in a pioneering article on Australian exploitation, it acts as a 'challenge to hegemonic notions of good taste'; because it guarantees the goodness of those who pass judgement; or because it lays bare the fraudulence of the cinematic illusion itself. In any case, the badness of exploitation would seem to have much in common with the badness Routt finds in Australian cinema.

But this is another story that *Mad Dog* does not entirely fit. Like Morgan himself, the film straddles the line between good and evil, redemption and damnation: excessive certainly, perhaps tasteless, but too arty and ambitious to be categorised as pure abject trash, or for that matter, as straightforward popular entertainment. Hartley himself seems aware of the issue: while *Not Quite Hollywood* grants *Mad Dog* two separate segments, they're devoted less to the film itself than to colourful anecdotes about Hopper's behaviour behind the scenes, including many retold here. Mora, who appears in *Not Quite Hollywood* as an interview subject, would recycle these anecdotes in the *Mad Dog* DVD commentary and in subsequent writings; they are now so routinely incorporated into discussion of *Mad Dog* it is as if the film, in all its ragged marginality, required this material in order to appear complete.

The more these anecdotes are repeated, the more it becomes clear that they constitute a coherent cycle, following the familiar pattern of the purgatorial narrative. Hopper starts the decade riding high on the global film scene, before paying the price for what would conventionally be viewed as a life of sin; via Peru and Taos, he descends to a strange netherworld which at best is 'not quite Hollywood', at worst its grotesque parody or inversion. Here he undergoes trial by flood and fire, and faces a series of challenges set for him by the locals: standing up to Jack Thompson, winning over David Gulpilil, fleeing from Frank Thring. His successful transformation into Morgan is signified by his arrest at the end of the shoot, after which he's literally pronounced dead, a low point which nevertheless gives rise to the possibility of rebirth; dispatched from the country at speed, he sets out on the long journey back to respectability and health.

Like many a hero of Antipodean cinema, Hopper in this story recreates himself by at least temporarily *becoming Australian*: travelling, it might be said, from Kansas to Oz. From this perspective, the central incident in the saga is clearly

Billy and Morgan in their cave.

Gulpilil's consultation with the trees and kookaburras, whose apparent tolerance puts Hopper ahead of most locals in terms of establishing a spiritual connection to the land. Whatever we finally make of this anecdote, we have Gulpilil's testimony to his fond relationship with Hopper, whom he later visited in the United States. As he tells the tale, art and life fused in accordance with Hopper's Method approach: 'I became Billy, and Morgan became my friend.'

Part of the background to this friendship was that Hopper and Gulpilil were both outsiders on the *Mad Dog* set. Mora, with his European background, might pass for an outsider as well; but in nearly all the anecdotes of the shoot, it's Hopper who plays the 'cringing' role, accepting a subordinate position with occasional protests ('We're not animals, man'). Despite his youth, Mora is the 'master' figure, who must tame the beast in Hopper or treat him as a child to be reassured, cajoled, hurried along. In short, this is a story in which Mora, the director, behaves like a coloniser, and Hopper, the actor, like a 'native'. All of which helps to account for what might otherwise seem puzzling: that almost no-one in *Not Quite Hollywood* embodies the home-grown wildness of Ozploitation as vividly as Hopper, the imported American star.

Almost no-one. The segments of *Not Quite Hollywood* devoted to *Mad Dog* form part of a celebration—half ironic, but only half—of a time before strictly enforced safety regulations, when filmmakers were boldly willing to risk the lives of cast and crew. To be sure, such filmmakers put themselves on the line as well, and *Not Quite Hollywood* tells their stories with particular relish: writer-director-star Sandy Harbutt brawling with the Hell's Angels during the making of his biker classic *Stone* (1974), or Trenchard-Smith appearing as a heavy in *The Man from Hong Kong* (1975) and getting beaten up on camera by his own imported star Jimmy Wang Yu.

Again a familiar pattern emerges: Hartley, like Weir in *Gallipoli*, is concerned to show how a group—in this case, the Australian filmmaking community—earned its stripes through risk, suffering and sacrifice. Routt's notion of a 'refusal' is relevant here: in the story told by *Not Quite Hollywood*, the supposed badness of Ozploitation serves as a means of defying artistic standards imposed from outside, belatedly escaping the chains of Empire. This escape is accomplished partly by a switch of allegiance from British to American cultural models, but above all through the selfless heroism of stuntmen—the ultimate foot soldiers of cinema, embodying virtues of athleticism and physical courage which from an Australian perspective seem the very opposite of 'art'.

This suggests one more allegorical interpretation of Morgan's dream, or rather of the behind-the-scenes footage captured by Elfick for *To Shoot a Mad Dog* and repurposed in *Not Quite Hollywood*. What the footage seems to show is a sacrificial rite, aimed at atoning for the guilt and shame of a traumatic colonial past. After a false start, Grant Page succeeds in fusing his identity with Hopper's, enacting Morgan's death and simultaneous rebirth in his backward leap from the cliff; afterwards, Hopper acknowledges him on camera as the greatest maniac of all.

'I have always had the feeling that Grant was indestructible', comments Trenchard-Smith as *Not Quite Hollywood* segues into its next round of yarns. Not only has Hartley incorporated Morgan's premonition of doom into a narrative of national redemption, he has amended the tragedy which was the starting point for *The Last Movie*, in which the stuntman played by Hopper failed to step in and save the lead. Funny things happen down under: Page sees it through, takes the fall where his American double cannot, and lives to tell the tale, like Orpheus returning from the underworld, or the risen Christ.

Epilogue: In Search of Morgan's Scrotum

Shortly after the Australian release of *Mad Dog*, the *Age* newspaper was contacted by a Mrs Philip Mims of Mentone in Melbourne, who said that the film had caused her deep distress. Not that she had seen it, or planned to. Rather, she took exception on behalf of her grandfather, the real Superintendent Cobham; in particular, she objected to the scene where Cobham orders the removal of Morgan's scrotum. Could an 'educated English gentleman', as Mrs Mims described her grandfather, possibly countenance such a thing?

Mrs Mims had to grant that yes, Morgan's body was mutilated, and yes, it happened on Cobham's watch. But the man himself was not to blame. 'It was not Cobham but the doctors who wanted all the bits and pieces.' What about the rumour that one of Cobham's descendents placed flowers every year on Morgan's grave? 'It is inconceivable that any member of the family would be sympathetic to Morgan.'

As Mrs Mims pointed out, the official report of the inquiry into the mutilation of Morgan's corpse contains no reference to the scrotum. Nor does the allegation appear in Carnegie's biography of Morgan. So how did it get into *Mad Dog*? Asked if she could shed any light on the matter, Carnegie explained that she had made a last-minute discovery while engaged in some further research into Morgan at the request of 'the film boys', who considered her published work 'a little hifalutin'.

Her later conclusions appear in a speech given to the Royal Historical Society of Victoria in November 1975 while *Mad Dog* was being shot. Here she suggests that the received view of Morgan as a brutal killer

> grew partly from a guilty feeling that the manner of his death
> was not legal, that he was in fact murdered, and… was partly
> a recoil from the horror engendered when it became known
> that his body had been barbarously mutilated.

The words echo in the mind, as if they referred to something much larger than the fate of one man; the point of view they express is, of course, exactly that of *Mad Dog* itself.

The newly-discovered source which Carnegie cited in her speech was the *Police History of Notorious Bushrangers of Victoria and New South Wales*, an unpublished work written in the early twentieth century by an Irish-Australian police officer named Martin Brennan, whose career began in the 1850s; a facsimile of the relevant manuscript passage appears in *Mad Dog*'s press kit, which is available as an extra on the Umbrella DVD. What it describes is a rumour, said to be current at the time, of 'tobacco pouches' (plural) being manufactured from portions of Morgan's 'tegument and scrotum'.[11]

Apart from this single clause, everything Brennan says about the treatment of Morgan's body is established fact; and some of the newspaper reports of the time have an undeniable euphemistic quality, as if hinting at matters too dreadful to be spelt out. On the other hand, Brennan makes no claim to have seen the pouches with his own eyes, and he has always had the reputation of a teller of tall tales: reviewing his *Reminiscences of the Gold Fields* in 1907, the *Sydney Morning Herald* complained that 'one does not know where reality ends, or where romance begins'.

Carnegie herself declined to comment further, beyond pointing out that 'old time squatters tanned and made articles from that portion of kangaroos'. For what it is worth, Professor John McQuilton, the author of Morgan's entry in the *Australian Dictionary of Biography*, has told me he is a believer. Given the systematic desecration of Morgan's body by Cobham and his associates, there is no reason to think they would shrink from this final outrage. Nor would it be surprising if witnesses kept their mouths shut.

There is one more thing to consider. Questioned further by the *Age*, Mrs Mims confessed that according to family tradition, there *was* a tobacco pouch. Cobham said it was made of calf skin, and perhaps it was; again, it depends which story you prefer. No doubt there are those even now who wish Morgan forgotten, scrotum and all. Personally, I like to think his ghost still lurks in the shadow of Hanging Rock, where he will continue to trouble visitors till the return of what is rightfully his.

ENDNOTES

1. The name 'Mad Dog Morgan' was unknown prior to the film (which was originally to be called simply *Mad Dog*, and reverted to that title when theatrically released in the US and UK). It has since come into wide use, even appearing on the plaque that marks Morgan's grave.

2. Kelly's story is told in numerous films starting with *The Story of The Kelly Gang* (1906), which is generally recognised as the first narrative feature ever made.

3. When I spoke to him in 2014, de la Manitou was at work on a film, *Along for the Ride*, that would chronicle his association with Hopper.

4. Australia's first Labor Prime Minister since 1949, Gough Whitlam was dismissed by the Governor-General, Sir John Kerr, on November 11 1975.

5. Hopper would play a traumatised Vietnam veteran on several occasions, starting with Henry Jaglom's *Tracks* (1977).

6. The quote is from the final speech of *Henry VI, Part III*, and is spoken by the character Gloucester as he continues to stab the corpse of the man he has just murdered.

7. *The Last Movie* appears on Rosenbaum's list of acid Westerns along with *The Shooting* (1966), *Glen and Randa* (1971) and *El Topo* (1970).

8. Outlaws in medieval England were said to 'bear the wolf's head', meaning that legally they were no longer considered human.

9. Waxworks at this period were associated with both pseudo-science and law enforcement. Philemon Sohier, co-founder of the Australia-wide Madame Sohiers waxwork chain, was also known as a leading 'phrenologist'; his business partner Maximilian Kreitmayer would eventually prepare the death mask of Ned Kelly.

10. That said, Mike Molloy strongly prefers the colour grading of the earlier DVD from Payless Entertainment.

11. 'Tegument' in this context simply means 'skin'.

BIBLIOGRAPHY

Note: This bibliography lists a selection of significant sources. Besides these, I've made use of archival materials obtained through the AFI Research Library and the National Library of Australia's Trove website (trove.nla.gov.au), as well as first-hand interviews.

Beilby, Peter, 'Production Preview: The Filming of Mad Dog', *Cinema Papers*, June–July 1976

Boldrewood, Rolf, *Robbery Under Arms* [1888]. Hawthorn: Lloyd O'Neil, 1970

Brophy, Philip, 'That's Exploitation!: Snobs', *FilmViews* no. 132, Melbourne, 1987

Carnegie, Margaret, *Morgan: The Bold Bushranger*. Melbourne: The Hawthorn Press, 1974

— 'The Death of Morgan the Bushranger', *Victorian Historical Magazine* no. 188, May 1977

Cocteau, Jean, *The Art of Cinema*, 1992, ed. and trans. Robin Buss. London: Marion Boyers, 1992

Collins, Felicity, 'History, Myth and Allegory in Australian Cinema', *Trames*, vol. 12, no. 3, 2008

Darrach, Brad, 'The Easy Rider in the Andes', *LIFE*, July 19, 1970

Forbes, Angus, 'Savage Waters— angle Dennis Hopper', *Critical Quarterly*, vol. 52, no. 3, 2010

Forscher, Helene, *Animals in the Landscape*, Gold Coast: Bond University, 2007, http://epublications.bond.edu.au/theses/forscher, accessed online 26 November 2014

Gibson, Ross, *The Diminishing Paradise: Changing Literary Perceptions of Australia*. Sydney: Angus and Robertson, 1984

Hoberman, J., *Dennis Hopper: From Method to Madness*. Minneapolis: Walker Arts Centre, 1988

Hollander, J., *Melodious Guile: Fictive Pattern in Poetic Language*. New Haven: Yale University Press, 1988

James, Nick, 'The S&S Interview: Jeremy Thomas, part one: The making of a super-producer', *Sight and Sound*, vol. 24, no. 4, April 2014

Laseur, Carol, 'Australian Exploitation Film: The Politics of Bad Taste', *Continuum: The Australian Journal of Media & Culture*, vol. 5 no. 2, 1990, ed. Adrian Martin

McFarlane, Brian, '*Mad Dog Morgan*', in *The Oxford Companion to Australian Film*, ed. Brian McFarlane, Geoff Mayer and Ina Bertrand. Melbourne: Oxford University Press, 1999

McQuilton, John, 'Morgan, Daniel (Dan) (1830–1865)', *Australian Dictionary of Biography*. Canberra: National Centre of Biography, http://adb.anu.edu.au/biography/morgan-daniel-dan-13109/text23717, first published in hardcopy 2005, accessed online 20 November 2014

Manwaring, W. H., 'Manuscript: Re Daniel Morgan Bushranger', *The La Trobe Journal*, no. 5, April 1970

Mora, Mirka, *Wicked But Virtuous*. Camberwell: Penguin, 2002

Mora, Philippe, '*Cops*: Buster Keaton', *Cinema Papers*, vol. 1 no. 2, November 1969

— 'Culture Shock: Australians in London in the Sixties', *Art Monthly*, no. 156, December 2002

— 'Mythology of Guts', *Cinema Papers*, vol. 1 no. 1, October 1969

— 'The Shooting of *Mad Dog Morgan*', The *Sydney Morning Herald*, January 31, 2010

— 'When Film Was Modern', *Art Monthly*, no. 152, August 2002

O'Regan, Tom, *Australian National Cinema*. New York: Routledge, 1996

Penzig, Edgar F., *Morgan the Murderer: A Definitive History of the Bushranger Dan Morgan*. Katoomba: Tranter Enterprises, 1989

Perez, Gilberto, *The Material Ghost: Films and their Medium*. John Hopkins: Baltimore, 1998

Rosenbaum, Jonathan, *Dead Man*. London: BFI Publishing, 2000

Routt, William D., 'Dad and Dave Come to Town', in *The Cinema of Australia and New Zealand*, ed. Geoff Mayer and Keith Beattie. New York: Wallflower Press, 2007

— 'Me Cobber, Ginger Mick: Stephano's Story and Resistance to Empire in Early Australian Film', in *Twin Peeks: Australian and New Zealand Feature Films*, ed. Deb Verhoeven. Melbourne: Damned Publishing, 1999

Seal, Graham, *The Outlaw Legend: A Cultural Tradition in Britain, America and Australia*. Cambridge: Cambridge University Press, 1996

Shead, Garry, 'Jesus Was An Outlaw', *Filmnews* vol. 6, no. 7, August 1976

Stead, Naomi, 'The Value of Ruins: Allegories of Destruction in Benjamin and Speer', *Form/Work: An Interdisciplinary Journal of the Built Environment*, no. 6, October 2003

Stratton, David, *The Last New Wave: The Australian Film Revival*. London: Angus & Robertson, 1980

Stuart, Amanda, 'The Dingo and Doomed Explorer Art', chapter from unpublished thesis *The Dingo in the Colonial Imagination*, available at Menzies Library, Australian National University, Canberra, 2013

Thoret, Jean-Baptiste, 'Dennis/Hopper, or The Man Who Was

Two and One', (trans. David Radzinowicz) in *Dennis Hopper and the New Hollywood*, ed. Matthieu Orlean. Paris: ESFP/ La Cinemathèque Française, 2009

Van de Klundert, Dominique, 'Sight & Mind: The Visualisation of Brain Function in the Collection of the Harry Brookes Allen Museum', Harry Brookes Allen Museum website, 2015, accessible online at http:// harrybrookesallenmuseum. mdhs.unimelb.edu.au/ publications

Weaver, Rachael, 'Waxwork', *Meanjin*, vol. 68 no. 3, spring 2009

Webb, Francis, *Collected Poems: Francis Webb*, ed. Toby Davidson. Crawley: UWA Publishing, 2011

Winkler, Peter L., *Dennis Hopper: The Wild Ride of a Hollywood Rebel*. Fort Lee: Barricade, 2011

Yeats, W. B., *The Collected Poems of W. B. Yeats*, ed. Richard J. Finneran. New York: Macmillan, 1989

FILMOGRAPHY

Absolutely Modern (Philippe Mora, 2012)

Alvin Purple (Tim Burstall, 1973)

The American Friend (Wim Wenders, 1977)

Apocalypse Now (Francis Ford Coppola, 1979)

Bad Boy Bubby (Rolf de Heer, 1993)

The Beast Within (Philippe Mora, 1982)

Ben-Hur (William Wyler, 1959)

Brother, Can You Spare a Dime (Philippe Mora, 1975)

The Chant of Jimmie Blacksmith (Fred Schepisi, 1978)

Chopper (Andrew Dominik, 2000)

Citizen Kane (Orson Welles, 1941)

Cops (Buster Keaton, 1922)

Easy Rider (Dennis Hopper, 1969)

El Topo (Alejandro Jodorowsky, 1970)

Gallipoli (Peter Weir, 1981)

The Gertrude Stein Mystery or Some Like It Art (Philippe Mora, 2010)

Glen and Randa (Jim McBride, 1971)

The Great Train Robbery (Edwin S. Porter, 1903)

Howling III—The Marsupials (Philippe Mora, 1987)

King of Kings (Nicholas Ray, 1961)

The Last Movie (Dennis Hopper, 1971)

The Left-Handed Gun (Arthur Penn, 1958)

Made in the U.S.A. (Jean-Luc Godard, 1966)

The Man from Hong Kong (Brian Trenchard-Smith, 1975)

The Man Who Shot Liberty Valance (John Ford, 1962)

Ned Kelly (Tony Richardson, 1970)

Not Reconciled (Jean-Marie Straub and Danièle Huillet, 1965)

Not Quite Hollywood: The Wild, Untold Story of Ozploitation (Mark Hartley, 2008)

Orphée (Jean Cocteau, 1950)

Picnic at Hanging Rock (Peter Weir, 1975)

Rebel Without A Cause (Nicholas Ray, 1955)

The Sentimental Bloke (Raymond Longford, 1919)

The Shooting (Monte Hellman, 1966)

The Shout (Jerzy Skolimowski, 1978)

Stone (Sandy Harbutt, 1974)

Swastika (Philippe Mora, 1974)

To Shoot a Mad Dog (David Elfick, 1976)

Tracks (Henry Jaglom, 1977)

Trouble in Molopolis (Philippe Mora, 1969)

Wake in Fright (Ted Kotcheff, 1971)

Walkabout (Nicolas Roeg, 1971)

CREDITS

Release year
1976

Production company
Motion Picture
Productions

Running time
102 minutes

Key crew

Producer
Jeremy Thomas

**Associate Producer/
Production Manager**
Richard Brennan

Director
Philippe Mora

Screenplay
Philippe Mora

Based on the book
*Morgan, The Bold
Bushranger* by
Margaret Carnegie

**Director of
Photography**
Mike Molloy

Camera Operator
John Seale

Editor
John Scott

**Production Design/
Art Direction**
Bob Hilditch

Costume Design
Bruce Finlayson

Music
Patrick Flynn

**Aboriginal Songs
and Didgeridoo**
David Gulpilil

**Production
Supervisor**
Peter Beilby

**Production
Coordinator**
Jenny Woods

Assistant Directors
Michael Lake, Chris
Maudson

Sound
Ken Hammond

Sound Re-recording
Peter Fenton

Stunts
Grant Page

Key cast

Daniel Morgan
Dennis Hopper

**Detective
Manwaring**
Jack Thompson

Billy
David Gulpilil

**Superintendent
Cobham**
Frank Thring

**Superintendent
Winch**
Michael Pate

Macpherson
Wallas Eaton

Sergeant Smith
Bill Hunter

Baylis
John Hargreaves

Wendlan
Martin Harris

Roget
Robin Ramsay

Italian Jack
Graeme Blundell

Barmaid
Liza Lee-Atkinson

Dr Dobbyn
Kurt Beimel

McLean
David Bracks

Judge Barry
Peter Collingwood

Gibson
Peter Cummins

Evans
John Derum

Martin
Gerry Duggan

Prisoner
Max Fairchild

Mrs Macpherson
Isobel Harley

John Evans
David John

Haley
David Mitchell

Maginnity
Grant Page

Watson
Philip Ross

Heriot
Bruce Spence

Bond
Ken Weaver

Acknowledgements

Countless people helped with this book, starting with Jane Mills, who commissioned it, Claire Grady and the team at Currency Press, and Philippe Mora himself, a constant source of inspiration and encouragement. Many *Mad Dog* veterans generously shared their memories or assisted in other ways: Graeme Blundell, Richard Brennan, David Elfick, Satya de la Manitou, Max Fairchild, Angus Forbes, David Gulpilil, Michael Lake, Mike Molloy, Grant Page, John Scott, and Jeremy Thomas. For discussion and support, I'm especially grateful to Jeremy Boland, Lesley Chow, Robert de Graaf, Sarah Flattley, Andrew Hart, Philippa Hawker, and Jeff Smith. Bill Routt gave crucial guidance via email, and my debt to his writing goes far beyond the places where he's quoted. The quote from Angus Forbes on page 24 appears with the kind permission of the author. Others who pointed the way through the labyrinth were Siobhan Dee, Maria-Elena Fieguth, Cathy Gallagher, Mark Hartley, Ryan Jefferies, John McQuilton, Kristy Matheson, Nathan Morris, Amanda Stuart, Lisa Sullivan, Dominique van de Klundert, and the staff of the AFI Research Library. I thank them all, as well as my family and, first and last, Nikki. All errors, misinterpretations and conscious untruths are my own. Finally, I would like to acknowledge the Wurundjeri people, the traditional custodians of the present site of Melbourne where this book was written, and the Wiradjuri people, of the area of southern New South Wales where much of *Mad Dog* was shot.

THE AUSTRALIAN SCREEN CLASSICS

'The Australian Screen Classics series is surely a must for any
Australian film buff's library.'
Phillip King, Royal Holloway, University of London

Alvin Purple by Catharine Lumby
ISBN 978 0 86819 844 6
Australia's first R-rated feature film created a furore when it was
released in 1973. Catharine Lumby revisits claims that the movie is
an exercise in sexploitation and argues the film's complexity.

The Back of Beyond by Sylvia Lawson
ISBN 978 0 86819 975 7
Representing the complex interrelations of the multicultural
community and their environs, *The Back of Beyond* is an exemplary
representation of 1950s Australian transformational culture.

The Barry McKenzie Movies by Tony Moore
ISBN 978 0 86819 748 7
An illuminating tribute to Bruce Beresford's subversive and
hilarious *The Adventures of Barry McKenzie*, and its riotous sequel, by
cultural historian and documentary-filmmaker, Tony Moore.

The Boys by Andrew Frost
ISBN 978 0 86819 862 0
Andrew Frost's monograph explores the achievements of this
award-winning film, placing its thematic concerns into a broader
context of social anxieties about violence, crime and morality.

The Chant of Jimmie Blacksmith by Henry Reynolds
ISBN 978 0 86819 824 8
Based on Thomas Keneally's award-winning novel, Fred Schepisi's
1978 film is a powerful and confronting story of a black man's
revenge against an injust and intolerant society.

The Devil's Playground by Christos Tsiolkas
ISBN 978 0 86819 671 8
Christos Tsiolkas invites you into Fred Schepisi's haunting film
about a thirteen-year-old boy struggling with life in a Catholic
seminary.

Jedda by Jane Mills
ISBN 978 0 86819 920 7
Jedda was one of several post-World War II melodramas dealing with miscegenation. Mills examines this and the representation of the Australian Aborigine with the Hollywood Western film genre.

The Mad Max Movies by Adrian Martin
ISBN 978 0 86819 670 1
Adrian Martin offers a new appreciation of these classics: '*No other Australian films have influenced world cinema and popular culture as widely and lastingly as George Miller's* Mad Max *movies*'.

The Piano by Gail Jones
ISBN 978 0 86819 799 9
Writer Gail Jones' thoughtful and perceptive critique of Jane Campion's award-winning film, *The Piano*, assesses the film's controversial visions, poetic power and capacity to alienate.

Puberty Blues by Nell Schofield
ISBN 978 0 86819 749 4
'Fish-faced moll', 'rooting machine', 'melting our tits off': with its raw dialogue, Bruce Beresford's *Puberty Blues* has become a cult classic. Nell Schofield takes a look at this much-loved film.

Rabbit-Proof Fence by Larissa Behrendt
ISBN 978 0 86819 910 8
Larissa Behrendt's honest and frank account of the film finds much that resonates: the need and desire to find one's home, one's sense of place and one's sense of self.

Wake in Fright by Tina Kaufman
ISBN 978 0 86819 864 4
Tina Kaufman's essay explores how *Wake in Fright* was received on its first release in 1971. She also discusses the film's discovery after being lost for over a decade and its second release in 2009.

Walkabout by Louis Nowra
ISBN 978 0 86819 700 5
Louis Nowra says *Walkabout* 'destroyed the cliché of the Dead Heart and made us Australians see it from a unique perspective'.

Available from all good bookshops or buy online at
www.currency.com.au